MY LIFE
with
LIFERS

Other Books by Dr. Elaine Leeder

The Gentle General: Rose Pesotta,
Anarchist and Labor Organizer

Treating Abuse in Families: A Feminist and
Community Approach

The Family in Global Perspective:
A Gendered Journey

Inside and Out:
Women, Prison and Therapy

Dr. Elaine Leeder

MY LIFE
with
LIFERS

Lessons For A Teacher:
Humanity Has No Bars

Terra Nova Books
SANTA FE, NEW MEXICO

Distributed by SCB Distributors, (800) 729-6423

Terra Nova Books

Published by Terra Nova Books, Santa Fe, New Mexico.
www.TerraNovaBooks.com

ISBN 978-1-938288-02-9

Contents

Acknowledgments

Although the words and ideas in this book are mine, many people have assisted in the process of bringing it to fruition. First, I must thank Jeanne Wall for suggesting that I write a book on my work in prisons. Then, Jim Malek furthered the process, editing and providing help in thinking through who my audience might be and how to convey this story. After the first drafts were completed, Connie Tuttle and Mary Cone provided excellent editorial advice. Kathy Barry, noted feminist author and activist, did another thorough read, making structural recommendations that were invaluable.

I must also thank the men of New Leaf on Life, who have provided me with the encouragement and advice on the details and content of this work. It is their situation and humanity that made me want to tell their stories in the first place. I also appreciate John Kelly, my co-leader, who has been my role model and buddy.

To the folks at San Quentin, my appreciation again. Thanks to Laura Bowman Salzsieder, Dr. Jody Lewen, and Sgt. Gabe Walters, Public Information Officer, for their input and support.

Enormous thanks to my friends Linda Evans, Eve Goldberg, Pam Adinoff, Sarah Jennings, Laurie Lippin, Ari Elster, Flora Lee Ganzler, Ilene Pearce, David Salm, Jann Nunn, Les and Judith Adler, Jo Ann Smith, Gale Kissen, and Maryana Plesh for being my support group and friendship circle. My East Coast friends remain my "family," and I am full of love for the years of devotion in our created community. Cleo Gorman, Ron Ackerman, David Schwartz, Anne Wexler, Tony Gaenslen, Yvonne Fogarty, Sandy Pollack, Mary Corsaro, Jerry Sirlin, Barbara Cartwright, Barbara Adams, Debbie Brown, Craig Longley,

Bob Armstrong, Ralph Siciliano, Peggy Williams, Sandra Herndon, Craig Pugh, Garry Brodhead, David Leeder, Sarah, Lavi, Farai, and Thandi Chidavaenzi, and so many others are why I can continue this work.

To my daughter, Abigail Leeder, and her partner, Arjen Hoekstra, my love and gratitude. To my colleagues at Sonoma State University, appreciation for the intellectual community that encourages scholarship as well as activism. I am privileged to work in such an academic setting. And to my staff, Karen Leitsch, Holly Sautner, and Julie Wood, thanks for all you do to make things work.

Most of all, I dedicate this book to the millions of incarcerated men and women in the world whose stories should be heard. As a society, we need to understand why they did what they did so that we can undo the causes that often led to their crimes and work on alternative solutions to incarceration.

Introduction

What's a Nice Girl Like You Doing in a Place Like This?

I have always been drawn to darkness and the dark side of people's lives. It may be because my father's family was killed in Lithuania during the Holocaust; it might also be because my mother's people were immigrants from Poland, with many of the troubles that immigrant families experienced, including poverty and mental illness.

My childhood home always had the shades drawn so the neighbors would not see what was going on inside. In my father's village in Lithuania, it was the neighbors who turned in the Jews and watched them being marched off to the pits where my family was shot and buried. My father spent his whole life remembering his dead mother, sister, and brother, and feeling survivor's guilt for having made it out alive before the war began.

Money had been sent for one family member to travel to the U.S. His sister was to go, but she decided to stay home to care for their elderly father. My own father was sent instead, with plans to pay the way for the rest of the family when he raised the money. But Hitler marched through Eastern Europe first, slaughtering millions. My family was among them. My father's faith in God was his only solace through tormented days and nights. He often sat late into the night reading Jewish religious tracts seeking the peace he could not find otherwise.

Whatever the cause of my being drawn to darkness, I know I always championed the underdog. In the first grade, a young African-American friend called for me on the second day of school, but my mother told me I could not walk with her or be her friend. I knew something was wrong with the way we dealt with the "other." To me, there was no "other"—she was my friend, and I would spend time with her, no matter what I was told.

This rebellion stayed with me through childhood, college, and later life. By the time I was in college, I had marched with Martin Luther King before his famous "I Have a Dream" speech. In Boston, where I went to school, there was a rich tradition of rebellion, and it was easy for me to find it. I smoked pot before it was "in," beginning as early as 1965. I joined civil rights and antiwar activities, and I was in a feminist consciousness-raising group as soon as such movements emerged. In these groups, I discovered that as a woman in a patriarchal society, I, too, was an underdog.

When I saw that I was discriminated against as a woman, I began to identify my dissatisfaction with the way things were in our society; I was tormented by social inequality, gender discrimination, class bias, racism, and militarism.

Having been raised an orthodox Jew, I knew about "doing good" in the world; it was part of a Jewish world view. These deeply instilled values taught me to love all human beings, to give charity, to wrong no one, to help a neighbor, to never take revenge, to embrace the stranger among us, to work for justice in the world, and to repair the "tear" in the universe by being a good human being. These values are called *mitzvoth*, part of the 613 commandments that Jews are supposed to follow. I might not have followed the religious rituals all my life, but they have governed my behavior as much as possible.

As a social worker in New York City, a therapist at mental hospitals and mental health clinics, and while working with alcoholics and drug addicts, I was fascinated by people who did not fit the norm. I always wondered how they could do it, since I tended to be someone who could not do much that was illegal. After many years of education and training, I became a college professor. I began to study deviance and its complexity, wanting to understand what drove people to do harm to others. At first, I began working with victims of domestic violence, but I was soon drawn to the perpetrators, to the challenge of their complicated minds. As a feminist, I felt it was my social obligation to work with people who caused pain to women. While working in a summer program for students about to enter college, some of them asked to visit a prison. I, too, was interested in such places, knowing that people there could help me understand perpetrators of domestic violence.

In 1995, in what was to be a pivotal moment in my career, I took the high school students to the Elmira Correctional Facility in upstate New York for a tour by the warden. I was struck by the cold, harsh facility and the fact that it was 150 years old. When the tour was over, I asked the warden if the inmates had any educational opportunities. He said they had only GED classes and some self-help programs like Alcoholics Anonymous (A.A.). In an impetuous moment of generosity, I offered to bring some college education programs inside. The warden was thrilled, and thus began my career with prisoners.

Several years later when I moved to California to become the dean of social sciences at Sonoma State University, I discovered a prison education program at San Quentin State Prison. Drawn once again to the dark side, I began volunteering there and was once again taken with the work because it was so gripping to find human connection in such a dark and miserable place.

When the class ended, a few prisoners who were my students asked if I would lead a group of lifers. I was flattered that they thought enough of me to have our own group. New Leaf on Life, a name chosen by the prisoners themselves, has continued since its inception in 2005. These men were sentenced to life in prison—with the possibility of parole—not to death in prison. And yet there they stay because of the attitudes and prejudices against them. Having paid their dues to society, most pose no risk to that society anymore, and many guards, educators, and administrators in prisons agree that they should be out. In California, it costs $46,000 a year to incarcerate a prisoner. Certainly, this money could be better spent elsewhere than for these men who no longer need to be there.

I am not writing here about those who are unable or unwilling to change, nor those who will continue to pose a risk to society. But they are the minority among those who are in for "life." Yet social policy often focuses on the young "gang bangers" who are doing short sentences, or on death row inmates who will never get out.

The experience in prison has set me on a new path of work. I have learned much from my students, perhaps even more than they gained from me. In this book, I share these lessons I have learned as I watch men inside begin the long and difficult process of redemption and transformation.

In my fifteen years' work in major prisons, I have spent much time in the darkness of life there, and I have seen many inmates come into the light as the process of change occurs. Many people have asked me details of my work with prisoners; thus, I have decided to document my experiences and highlight some of the men with whom I have had the privilege of working. Most of these men have committed terrible crimes, crimes for which they have been sentenced to long terms. Many have served at least the minimum necessary for parole, but still they remain in prison because of the nature of parole and "get tough on crime" views that make it impossible for men who are ready to be released to begin life outside.

Public policy and social change efforts need to distinguish among groups of prisoners and see that they cannot be generalized; each category has its own risks, challenges, and policy issues.

How many of us outside drive by prisons rarely thinking of the warehousing of humanity taking place behind those walls? Before I went into a prison, I thought everyone there deserved to be there—they belonged inside; the experience of prison was good for them, punishing them for what they had done. Once inside, I have learned about the real people, with real stories and reasons for doing what they did.

In this book, I will tell you some of these stories, since every one is different. Though they have committed terrible crimes, these are not evil people. For the most part, they are aware of and disturbed by what they did. I have learned that each one has a family traumatized by his crimes, as the victims and their families have been. Most are remorseful for what they did, and often want to make amends to the victims, their families, and the community they have harmed.

These are thoughts often not conveyed to the larger society, which watches "Lockup" and thinks everyone inside is a predator, and that violence is a daily experience in prison life. Many in our society enjoy seeing others suffer; thus, we watch such shows catering to our prurient interests. Just remember how we were all glued to the television during the 9/11 attacks, watching people jump from the burning towers. Often, we think no further about such shows after we turn off the TV. Now, I have learned that there is more to what goes on in prison than is covered by movies and TV.

I also have learned there is little to no rehabilitation in prisons, and that if a prisoner is to transform, it is done through sheer grit and determination—succeeding in spite of the system, not because of it. I have learned that people who commit crimes can change, and that many of them could do more good on the outside working with young people. These men were once directionless kids in gangs, often in trouble. Sure, there are inmates I would never want to see on the streets, but they are the minority. In fact, the U.S. Department of Justice estimates that 95 percent of those who are incarcerated will be eventually discharged. Therefore, it is imperative as a society that we do something for these prisoners so they can become contributing members of our world.

In the following pages, I will tell you about my experiences inside prisons and what I have learned working with this population, as well as suggest some policy changes that are badly needed. Having taught sociology for many years, I know about social problems from the inside out.

The mass incarceration we in the U.S. are living with now, particularly of people of color, can be considered the newest form of slavery. Angela Davis argues in her book *Are Prisons Obsolete?* (Seven Stories Press, 2003) that this incarceration binge is a contemporary manifestation of the racialized disparities that many of us believe were abolished in 1865. In fact, more black men are in prison now than lived under slavery. From 1990 to 2003, African-Americans made up the majority of the increase in incarceration, with the number of imprisoned blacks jumping 76.2 percent from 360,000 to 621,000 (Wright J., 2006). Now, 3.5 percent of all black males are in prison, and more than 10 percent in the 25-29 age group (p. 316). More black men are in prison than attending college. This increase is in stark contrast to the fact that the numbers of violent crimes is decreasing at the same time! In the U.S. today, there is a movement toward decarceration. The prisoner rights movement is advocating alternatives to incarceration—restorative justice and reconciliation rather than building more prisons. It seems undeniable that economic and racial disparities are major contributors to crime, that lack of opportunity leads people to meet their needs illegally. We could take major steps toward decarceration and its many benefits if our society sought solutions to poverty and an end to both the gross inequalities in our public education system and the criminalization of drugs. My experiences with men in prison have taught me that change is possible. Here is my story and theirs.

Chapter 1

Breaking Into Prison: Elmira Correctional Facility

In 1995, I began teaching a lecture series sponsored by Ithaca College. Once a week, I went to Elmira Correctional Facility and taught the inmates Introduction to Sociology. Sometimes, other college professors would help. The students all had been convicted of felonies. Some were lifers who were still there even though parole was possible; others had determinate sentences that would allow them to be released eventually. It was a maximum-security prison, and these men were considered dangerous, although I never saw any hostile behavior.

At first, I was frightened, thinking that my life might be in danger. But soon, I realized that the guys were thrilled to have me there, helping them break the monotony while using their brains for something other than the mundane daily activities of prison life. They often told me that if anything were to happen while I was there, they would protect me. One night, I remember hearing an altercation in the yard below our classroom window. The guards arrived and told us to remain in the room until the fighting ended. I was frightened, but my guys—all thirty of them—promised me I would be protected. In fact, I could not have been safer, since the students did not want the program to end and would do all they could to keep me coming back.

Elmira Correctional Facility has a long and colorful past, beginning when the New York State Legislature voted to build a new prison for first-time offenders ages 16-30 on the site of a former prison camp.

The prison, which officially received its first inmates from Auburn Prison in July 1876, was the first "reformatory," beginning a new era in the science of penology. The harsh methods of the "Auburn" and "Pennsylvania Systems," including corporal punishment, striped uniforms, and lockstep marching, were rejected along with the earlier reforms fostered by the Quakers in Pennsylvania. The Quakers had long been advocates of more-humane prison conditions, having experienced their own history of incarceration because of their religious views. An early Quaker prison reformer, Elizabeth Fry, urged changes at Newgate Prison in London, and many of her recommendations for rehabilitative measures in prison became law in England.

Under Elmira's first warden, Zebulon Brockway, who served for twenty-four years, imprisonment was designed to reform each inmate through an individualized program. Brockway rejected pointless hard labor, a regimen of silence, religious and morality lectures, and strict obedience enforced by brutality. Among the programs begun at the reformatory were courses in ethics and religion, vocational training in various trades, and extracurricular activities such as a prison band, newspaper, and athletic leagues. Each morning, there was tutoring and remediation, individual diets and calisthenics were introduced, and everyone had an individualized education file.

There were even hot and cold baths and Swedish massage for a short time (www.ceanational.org/aboutce/history.htm).

Influenced by the methods of Walter Crofton's "Irish system" as well as Alexander Maconochie's experiments in Australian penal colonies, discipline was largely patterned after military academies, with inmates dressed in military-style uniforms and often marching to the tune of a fife-and-bugle band.

Inmates would be classified by three "grades," with new prisoners at the second grade for their first six months. The most responsive and cooperative prisoners earned a first grade, with the opportunity for additional privileges or "marks" that could include parole or a reduction of sentence. Inmates also could be demoted for failing in their duties, while those who were less responsive to rehabilitation or had behavioral problems were placed at the third grade.

However, under such a program of indeterminate sentencing, tension was often high among the general population, as prisoners were rarely told how long their imprisonment would last, and Brockway later increased the facility's use of corporal punishment. After several prisoners were transferred to mental asylums, some people questioned the success of the reformatory system.

Still, Elmira's program was influential in prison reform. Two central ideas emerged: differentiating between juvenile and adult offenders, and acknowledging the possibility of prisoner rehabilitation.

Despite its mixed results, the Elmira Reformatory would influence the construction of twenty-five similar institutions in twelve states over the next quarter-century, reaching its height in 1910. Although the education programs that Elmira introduced were the first to serve inmates in a correctional facility, most of the teaching staff was often unqualified, and the complex system of classifying prisoners by grades made progress difficult to maintain. Eventually, all well-behaved inmates were placed in the first grade, with a few in the second grade and those under punishment in the third grade.

However, after Brockway's resignation, the reformatory reverted to standard custody and treatment methods, and eventually became the Elmira Correctional and Reception Center, an adult maximum-security prison holding approximately 1,800 inmates.

By the time I got there in 1995, the facility was decayed and crumbling. Outside was a statue of an older man with his hand on the shoulder of a youth, both looking off into the distance of the rolling Chemung County hills. In winter, the buildings were drafty, cold, and inhospitable. In summer, inmates tried to tame the surroundings a bit by planting a garden of flowers and vegetables. For the most part, the prison looked exactly like what one might expect: doors clanging shut, guards with heavy key rings, and prisoners in green looking as if they had reached the ends of the Earth.

The education building was far from the main gate. So after being searched thoroughly, we would wait to be escorted in by the guards, who would walk us across the yard and unlock each of our classrooms. Often, I was the only educator in a group of twenty volunteers. Others were from A.A., Narcotics Anonymous (N.A.), religious organizations, and other groups usually affiliated with a religious denomination.

At first, I was apprehensive, sitting in a room with convicted felons. After all, I was a woman alone in an all-male maximum-security detention facility. I wondered what I was doing there and why I had chosen this path. Later, I began to experience empathy for these men's lives and their paths to prison. Those who first came to my group were self-selected, having been told only that a college class would be offered by a professor from Ithaca College. In my first session, there were twenty-five men. Later, others joined, having heard from their friends that something was happening on Tuesday nights in Education. I conducted the classes as I would any other. A number of the students had GED educations and could read and comment on what they read. Writing was more problematic since none of them had formal training in it. Although I assigned readings, I found that discussions were the most provocative. The students could relate to the readings about racism, power differences in society, and violence. The discussions were lively, and many of the men could speak from their life experience about the topic of the day. I might lecture on family violence, and then they would tell of their experiences first as victims of child abuse and then as perpetrators of wife battering.

In one lecture, I remember distinguishing between wife beaters who could be called "Pit Bulls" and those who were "Cobras." The students differed with the author of the work we were discussing because they believed a perpetrator was not one or the other but that there was a transition. They felt a man went from being tenacious and fearful of losing his partner (a Pit Bull) to becoming a Cobra (a cold-blooded, heartless perpetrator). This was certainly a position that neither I nor the author had ever considered.

My students were highly enthusiastic participants. One, called Great Mind because of his philosophizing approach to life, was a tall, striking, African-American man from New York City who had been in prison since he was nineteen. He was now in his early thirties and had been in a number of the state's penitentiaries, studying religion and philosophy as well as body building there. Great Mind was the scholar of the group, often gently challenging the others to think more deeply about a subject. His family had supported him throughout his incarceration, and sent him mail and funds regularly. Years later, Great Mind was finally paroled and is now working in finance in New York City. He is doing well and is about to begin a college program, his good behavior finally having earned him a chance outside.

While in prison for a felony, Great Mind wrote a short essay about the impact of the college program on his life. In it, he said he felt that he was living in a "sub-cultural society that was governed by a systematic order of strict rules and dehumanizing norms." He really emphasized that an inmate must seek rehabilitation "administered by the determination within the self" as well as redemption—"setting free of the self from the personally constructed prison of one's own wrongs, mishaps, poor judgments, and bad decision-making." Great Mind also emphasized the need to become educated because if one "already excelled academically, then knowing the self would be the path to self-taught education."

He used all three—rehabilitation, redemption, and education—at different points and found that the college experience became "my escape from an underworld of pain, madness, and inner chaos." He also said that "this new-found education became my temple of reasoning and place of clarity." And Great Mind saw that it had a similar effect as well on other prisoners "who were blessed to have the same opportunity and took advantage of it." But even more important than the learning, he said, was the fact that "the most rewarding aspect of the program was indeed the human element, the interaction between the prisoner and the faculty members."

He noted that "these people had to go through a long, unwarranted, and discouraging screening process just to get into the prison. I often told the other prisoners who questioned me about the program that the professors had to break into the prison so they could teach us voluntarily." Great Mind was thankful to those who invested in the prisoners, saying that they had "endured a lot to reach out and touch some of the ones who most of society has written off as failures." Finally, he said, "through their sacrifices, I've come to understand that, 'To whom much is given, much is required.' "

Another of our students, Robin Hughes, was incarcerated in 1996 for murder, robbery, and possession of a controlled substance. He is still serving a fifteen-years-to-life sentence. He was so inspired by our program that he enrolled in college classes at another prison once he left Elmira, and was featured on a "60 Minutes" episode because of his dedication to the Bard College education program in New York State prisons. He is now at Clinton Correctional Facility, which is minimum security, but said on "60 Minutes" that he would happily go back to a maximum-security facility to attend the Bard program where he was intellectually challenged.

The Bard classes operate in three maximum-security prisons and two medium-security transitional facilities. They educate two hundred male and female prisoners in a rigorous full-time program offering both an associate's degree and a bachelor's degree. Students from Bard work with the college's faculty and attend classes inside with the prisoners, in a unique way of educating both populations.

In my own program, it was fascinating to watch Robin and Great Mind debate in the class. Once, at an event honoring the prison's volunteers, these, my favorite two students, gave me an award for dedication to education inside. I still have a photo of them together smiling at the event. The discussions in their class were more evocative than any others I've ever had in thirty-five years of teaching at the college level. The students would talk of prison life, philosophers, and sociologists they had read, and weave their discussions through with street language and a remarkable command of the lexicon of intellectual discourse. It was a sight to behold, and I often felt out of my league in these discussions.

Another prisoner, Seluh Tsarek, served ten years for manslaughter in the killing of his mother in 1997. His father was a professional, and the family was quite accomplished, having emigrated from Eritrea. Seluh's incarceration humiliated the family, but his skill as a student served him well inside. He wrote well-honed and well-argued papers, and enrolled in community college programs after being paroled. He is eager to earn a degree in film studies, and document the experience of incarceration.

I would often invite other college professors from Ithaca to accompany me to my classes and also to teach one of their own. My colleagues were amazed at the high level of intellectual engagement shown during those classes. Many said the classes were far better than any others they had taught, even at graduate levels and Ivy League colleges. The incarcerated men were bright, intelligent, and had amazing street smarts. What they lacked was the formal education needed to make it in the outside world. Some of them told me they had taken to crime because of their failures at school.

One man, whom I will call Bill, described an incident from his elementary school days. He had been assigned to read a paragraph aloud to the class. After he finished, the teacher chastised him in public for having read the wrong paragraph. He left school that day, he remembered, and began to break windows as a result of his anger. Soon, he began spending time with other juvenile delinquents, and the rest is history. Not much later, he was placed in a juvenile detention facility and started down the road of crime. Although that one teacher cannot be blamed, certainly this inmate's failure at school was one component of his path to crime.

Another time, I invited a business professor to speak on investments and financial security. The interest of these hard-core prisoners from tough and poor backgrounds amazed me as he spoke of the market and showed the prisoners how to read the stock page of the *Wall Street Journal*, having brought with him enough for all the students. There is a photo of this intellectual-looking, white professor standing over a brawny black man in a green uniform, showing him how to read the stock tables. It is an image that will remain with me forever because it proved to me that all prisoners are capable of being challenged and educated. That professor told me that watching this man being welcomed to the world of finance was one of the intellectual high points of his career. The prisoner decided to try investing through members of his family. With small amounts of money that he sent home, they played the market for him based on his recommendations.

Soon after beginning these groups, I invited a colleague to assist me, and Brian Nance, an African-American university admissions director, was eager to participate. I needed help in booking speakers and working with the men, as well as company for the hour's drive on those cold, snowy nights on upstate New York roads. Brian became an invaluable ally, bringing a cultural understanding that I, as a middle-aged, white woman, did not have. Guys resonated with him, and he was able to lead provocative and intense conversations. When I moved to California, I was pleased that Brian took over the program along with Dr. Naeem Inayatullah, a political science professor, and Dr. David Shapiro, a professor of communications. They kept it going for another three years until Ithaca College discontinued the program because of political machinations.

A college program remained at the prison, since Binghamton University had been operating there as well for a time, but there is no longer any program there. However, Cornell University offers programs at Auburn Correctional Facility and Cayuga Correctional Facility, which are not too far from Elmira. In the Cornell program, students are taught by professors and graduate students, and an associate's degree is awarded from Cayuga Community College. That program has been going for ten years through Cornell's Extended Education and Summer Sessions program.

My experience at Elmira, although only six years, gave me an experience that I knew I wanted to replicate upon moving to California. Seeing human beings kept in cages like zoo animals had had a profound impact in setting my future path. I saw their minds unchallenged; I saw a tragic waste of humanity. I felt as if I had stepped into the belly of the beast when I entered prison education, and somehow was providing a bit of light in a very dark and hostile place.

In my classroom, the prisoners were treated like any other student, regardless of their crimes or previous lifestyles. Though I met people so unlike myself, I marveled to discover our similarities. They all had families, some of whom remained loyal through their incarceration. Some had been abandoned, and they found educational opportunity a reassuring sign that someone on the outside cared for them. We were similar in our aspirations and our need to feel good about something in ourselves.

This education process was a chance for me, an immigrant's daughter, to show that the path through education can lead to a fuller, richer life than they had ever imagined. For me, it was a profound experience to feel their hope, fears, joy, laughter, and pain. That empathy surprised me: How could I actually come to care for people who had murdered or kidnapped others? It proved easy—because these are real people, with the same complement of emotions that we all share. Their lives had been horrible, with abuse and violence part of the daily experience. Their prison lives are more drab and painful than ours, but they are people nonetheless.

We share much in common, and we each have much to learn from the other. The people I am writing about have developed insight, self-awareness, and a desire to make a difference in the world. They are quite unlike the folks for whom prison is just a training ground for more violence and drug addiction. I am working with people who are just like you or me; they are locked up, but they have transformed themselves. You and I need to know them, and to know that redemption is possible and does take place.

Chapter 2

Redemption Through Education:
San Quentin State Prison

After I became a dean at Sonoma State University in Northern California in 2001, I began to explore programs in prison, knowing I needed to remain involved with the work that had added so much meaning to my life. Soon, a friend told me about the Prison University Project (PUP), a Patten University program at San Quentin (SQ) run by Jody Lewen. I contacted Dr. Lewen and discovered that volunteer faculty members from the San Francisco Bay Area staffed an associate's degree program there which had been started after the Violent Crime Control and Law Enforcement Act barred people who were incarcerated from receiving Pell Grants, pretty much ending higher education in prisons and leading to the shutdown of almost 350 programs nationally (www.prisonuniversityproject.org).

Initiated by a professor from the University of California at Davis, the Education Department at SQ and Patten University of Oakland negotiated to begin a program, which started in the fall of 1996 with just two classes, no budget, and a volunteer coordinator (www.prisonuniversityproject.org). Since then, the program has expanded and now offers approximately nineteen classes each semester to over three hundred men at San Quentin. It is an extension site of Patten University, an accredited independent university, and is the only on-site college program in all of the thirty-two state prisons in California. It receives no state or federal funding, and all the professors are volunteers from local universities. The program, which is run by an executive director, a program manager, an operations manager, and a part-time program assistant, is funded by donations, and the textbooks are donated by the publishers.

The 130 volunteer instructors, tutors, and office interns all contribute from four to ten hours a week each semester. In addition, the staff and volunteers give public educational programs, organize cultural events, teach, lecture, and publish on topics related to prisoner education. The project also aims to "challenge popular myths and stereotypes about people in prison, to publicly raise fundamental questions about the practice of incarceration, and to incubate and disseminate alternative concepts of justice, both within and beyond the academy" (www.prisonuniversityproject.org).

Because many students in the program are not ready for college-level work, a College Preparatory Program is associated with it. Since participants must have a high school diploma or a GED, many of those who need the preparation spend a year studying math and English to prepare for the rigor demanded in the associate's degree program.

I was thrilled to find this program, and began to volunteer immediately. I offered to teach Introduction to Sociology, and thus, I began my once-a-week commute to San Quentin with exhilaration and a bit of trepidation. To enter the prison on a regular basis, one has to obtain a "Brown Card," attesting that the volunteer has been trained on safety and security procedures as well as proper etiquette for interacting with prisoners. An annual training is required as well as yearly tuberculosis tests. I willingly submitted to these requirements, and joined the ranks of the three thousand volunteers who go to San Quentin on a regular basis.

My first trip there was frightening. I had heard about the prison for years, had driven by it often, and was intimidated by its imposing facade and harsh, austere appearance. San Quentin opened in July of 1852, and has a reputation as one of the most brutal prisons in the country. The thirty prisoners who built it were housed on a wooden ship in San Francisco Bay during construction. A dungeon remains on the site where inmates were tortured until the practice was banned in 1944. The prison is the oldest in the state and the only one with a death row. The gas chamber has not been used since 1996, since executions are now done by lethal injection.

It is ironic that the huge facility sits on a lovely piece of land overlooking San Francisco Bay. As I write, the prison holds over five thousand inmates even though it is designed for approximately three thousand. The facility has a reception center where new prisoners are processed as well as an open dormitory setting for level one, the lowest security level, and cellblocks for level two and three prisoners. Level four prisoners, the most violent, are not held at San Quentin. All prisoners are classified based on an assessment of education, level of violence, gang affiliation, and other markers.

A 2005 court order noted that the facility was "old, antiquated, poorly staffed, poorly maintained with inadequate medical space and equipment." Since then, the U.S. Supreme Court has ruled in a series of lawsuits that San Quentin and California's other prisons must discharge thirty-three thousand prisoners over the next few years because of conditions like these. Though the system was built to accommodate eighty thousand, there are now over one hundred thirty-three thousand prisoners in California. In the court's most recent decision on the subject, Justice Anthony Kennedy wrote: "A prison that deprives prisoners of basic sustenance, including adequate medical care, is incompatible with the concept of human dignity and has no place in a civilized society."

San Quentin's death row is the largest in the Western Hemisphere, holding over 637 male prisoners. Even Florida and Texas, which execute more prisoners, have fewer people on death row than San Quentin, where prisoners stay longer because of their appeals. Because the law requires that they have quick access to the court system for appeals and stays of execution, all California executions must occur at San Quentin.

In 2007, there was much consternation among lawmakers when it was discovered that the California Department of Corrections and Rehabilitation (CDCR) was building a new execution chamber, which it tried to keep secret. Though the state eventually allocated funds to complete the project, the chamber has yet to be used because of legal maneuvering and court efforts to curtail executions in California. From 1996 to 2007, eleven people were executed at SQ. From 1894 to 1937, 214 were executed by hanging, and after that, 196 were killed in the gas chamber. With all this in mind, death row looms over the prison, adding an aura of fear and sadness even in the bright California sunlight that often shines over this depressing place.

With this knowledge, I walked up to the gate for the first time in 2003 wondering, once again, what I was getting myself into. There are a series of four gates one must pass through before entering the prison grounds. At the first, you sign in and get your Brown Card. At the second, you sign in and get wanded (as might happen at an airport) to be sure you are carrying no weapons or contraband. At the third gate, you show your card for final entry. Once these are passed, you are waved through a final gate and enter the courtyard. It is imperative that you not wear denim or any color worn by the prisoners or guards: blue, yellow, green, or orange; a volunteer must stand out. If you come to the first gate with any of these colors on, you are turned away for the day. The prison's policy is that if you are taken hostage, the guards will not negotiate for your release. Although the situation has never arisen, the thought is daunting.

Being inside the grounds is almost surreal. To the right is a series of chapels, the largest being the Catholic one, then the Protestant, then the Native American office, and finally a smaller chapel ironically—and wonderfully—shared by Muslims and Jews. To the left is the Adjustment Center, where many of the most difficult prisoners are kept. This first courtyard is actually quite lovely, with a fountain where baby ducks and their mother have been known to nest; there are flowers and a flagpole in a well-landscaped area near the chapels. Directly in front of a viewer standing by the fountain is the old hospital built in the late 1880s; the new hospital, built around the old facade, looks like a state-of-the-art setting. Directly in front of the hospital is the prison's hub of activity, Four Post, a center for the guards where the watch commander is stationed.

As one walks down the ramp to the lower yard, directly under the new hospital is a historic place: the original dungeon built when the prison was constructed. Peering in is frightening; the cells are dark and dank, with smells from years past and places where shackles were hung from the wall. It reminds the viewer of exactly where we are and what goes on at San Quentin and other prisons like it. This is not a Hollywood movie, not a stage set, and not reality TV. This is *life*, and a horrific place to visit.

Often, a person going to a classroom may encounter two or three guards walking a group of prisoners in a gang to a new location. Prisoners are distinguished by their garb. The "mainliners," who have been sentenced and will be there for a while, are clad in denim pants and blue shirts. The new inmates, those still in reception, have on orange jumpsuits. In the event of rain, all the prisoners wear yellow slickers, and the guards don drab green, with keys and chains dangling.

After passing the dungeon, on the right is "Industries," the factory where much of the furniture used at institutions throughout California is made. In fact, dorm rooms at my university are furnished with beds, chairs, and dressers from "Industries." Prisoners working there earn pennies a day, which they use to buy food at the commissary once a week. "Industries" gives prisoners some activity so they are not all forced to stay in their cells continuously. They are encouraged to work during the day as factory laborers, clerks, or janitors, go to school, or exercise during their time off.

As we pass "Industries," we enter the lower yard. Here, prisoners segregate themselves based on ethnic and racial affiliations. To the right is the Asian group; left of them are the Norteños, and then the Mexicans unaffiliated with them or any other gang; next are the whites, and then the African-Americans, who have the most space because there are more of them in the facility. The groups do not mix in public, nor are the cells integrated. The only way one can share space with a friend of another background is in classrooms or activities; otherwise, all activity is racially divided. Some inmates and the prison administration say this is self-selected; others argue that it is how the guards keep the peace, and that the groups are separated so they can't unite against the administration.

After passing this "gauntlet" between all the groups working out, one enters a portable building called "Education." Before the portables were introduced about five years ago, classes were housed down a long flight of stairs in the dank rooms of the old education building, constructed when the prison came into existence. These new classrooms are better, but there are just not enough of them. Thus, classes occasionally are forced to function in the old laundry, with open ceilings and poor soundproofing. Many times, a class is in session while screaming and shouting next door—perhaps a group doing theater games—distracts students and instructor from the work at hand: trying to teach and learn. The desks are old and battered, and the whiteboards often do not have markers with which to write. The physical setting is rarely conducive to good process; nonetheless, it is the best the prison can do, so we take what we can get.

My first class, in the old education building, comprised twenty-five students who had been in the Prison University Project for a few years. All of them had taken English 99 to prepare for the many writing assignments. I was amazed at the quality of the discussion and the level of writing ability. Even though these men had noisy conditions in which to do their homework, the quality was better than that of many students I taught at the university. In addition, the quality of the discussion was far more in-depth and intelligent than any I had found before in many years of college teaching.

Those involved in correctional education have outlined the experience of "culture shock" that prison teachers undergo (Wright, R., 2005). Often, they feel the "heavy weight" of the prison walls and towers—the architecture conveying a sense that we are "in another place." The surly guards help us feel demeaned and insulted, and we often are confused by the varying ways they enforce prison policies. Once, I was sent home because I was wearing open-toed shoes, which are not allowed, although I had worn the same shoes three times before. Another time, when I brought a group of students in for a visit, the guard who asked why we were there would not let me answer and told me to "keep quiet" while he challenged my students. Clearly, the prison setting is unlike any other in which we have ever taught. There are stages in which new teachers feel like visitors, tourists, strangers, or settlers (p. 21). In such a place, we are part of a "fear-based culture," with a code of silence and intimidation. This is not usually how we run our classes, and thus, our cultures collide.

The process of becoming part of places like this moves a person beyond being a tourist, which is much like the honeymoon phase when everything is exciting and new (and intimidating) and the impressions are sometimes shocking (p. 28). Then, the teacher becomes like an exile, one who is marginal and thus feels different and has a sense of disintegration. Actually, one might even feel anxiety, anger, or withdrawal because the setting is so foreign and different from the familiar. Then comes reintegration, where the teacher finds it easier to function in this kind of setting, although always negotiating the boundaries and coping with the stresses (p. 29). Finally, someone who is going to remain teaching in prison becomes like a "settler," adjusting to the new culture and settling in by making the commitment to stay. It is not an easy process and may take months or years. I can honestly say that my process took a while, but it made me a settler in this alternative community. I am now completely at home.

I also had two teaching assistants (TAs) who worked with the men when class was not in session, and much later, they wrote an excellent essay titled "Sociologists Behind Bars." In it, Jody Short and Elizabeth Durgin, both graduate students then at the University of California at Berkeley, said: "In this unique environment, the students taught us as much about being sociologists as we taught them about sociology." Jody and Elizabeth clearly were going through the process of "culture shock" as they assimilated themselves into this foreign world. Later, they said of the prisoners: "They told us that we had simply supplied the terminology for what they already knew. Notably, they found this naming and categorizing of their experience empowering rather than oppressive. One student said that it was like clearing the fog from a clouded mirror."

The teaching assistants were amazed that "one student said he most appreciated learning about socialization and the impact of labels, and he told us that since taking the class, he had been talking to his son about these concepts, hoping to put him on a different path." The TAs were impressed that inmates conceived of themselves as "individuals with choice and agency" even in such a setting, and that many of the men maintained "a distinctive personality, style, and perspective even in the stifling prison environment." And they also were struck by how the students understood the "social construction of race and class, but gender differences continued to seem 'natural' to them." The TAs were disappointed, as women and as instructors, "to see many of the students persist in naturalized and stereotypical perceptions of men and women even as they saw how other categories were socially constructed."

Finally, the TAs were "deeply inspired in ways [the inmates] could never know. They were extraordinary students. They were, in short, dedicated scholars who demonstrated a level of engagement we have not witnessed in any other classroom setting. Their drive and thirst for knowledge was all the more remarkable because many of our students were serving life terms and had seemingly little to gain from slogging through coursework. They had found in education a source of meaning that animated their lives."

The thing needed most when teaching in prison is flexibility. At any given moment, the electricity might go out, a guard may come in and dismiss the whole class for security reasons, or some-one you don't know may just enter the room to sit and watch without permission. My interaction with the guards has always been cordial, but I make it a point to always do as they say, since they can control access to the room, not allow my students to attend, or exert their power in any number of ways. One must be creative as well, since we are not allowed to show DVDs or use PowerPoint teaching tools. To use teaching aids, you must submit them ahead of time, which is often problematic and sometimes not worth the trouble.

It is the power of the classroom interaction that is the profound experience. Inside, there are just plain old whiteboards, lectures, and discussions—never any fancy or up-to-date methodologies. Attendance can also become problematic; a prisoner might miss class because he is detained for disciplinary reasons. Others might be transferred in the middle of a semester, or a whole class may be canceled because the prison is on lockdown. One has to be an "old school" teacher in such a setting, focused on lecturing, discussion, and small group participation rather than using more-modern methods or aids.

For me, my classes were remarkable. The discussions were deeper and fuller than classroom experiences in the non-prison world. When I taught about self-fulfilling prophesies, the prisoners began to understand that they had been labeled and taught to become gang-bangers and trouble-makers early in life. When I taught about family violence, they told stories of their abuse as children and their own abuse of their wives and girlfriends. I saw their eyes open to the social realities that lead men to victimize those less powerful than themselves. They began to realize how they had victimized their families—and not just by committing the crimes that brought them to prison. I was able as a feminist to introduce the concept of male power, and they could understand it in relation to their experiences as powerless prisoners. At many stages in the discussions, I could see the light bulb going on over someone's head. One man talked about developing a critical awareness of the social stratification system and his own position in it. He saw that as a person of color, he had few choices available when he was young; he learned that prison was a continuation of the discrimination he had experienced since he was a child in public schools. This young man was the smartest student I had ever encountered. He wrote articulate and well-argued papers. Recently paroled, in part because of his exemplary behavior in prison, he is now a sociology major at San Francisco State University. The class opened his eyes to a discipline that could explain his experience, and empowered him to write, think, and act based on his knowledge. He now lectures in my class at the university, where he relates well to the students, whom I still ask to read the same books and write the same kinds of papers that he did.

In prison, most of life is segregated based on skin color and gang affiliation. But in the classroom, all those distinctions are erased, and the students relate to each other as peers. It is remarkable to watch people of different colors and races interacting as scholars, debating ideas, helping each other with papers, explaining concepts and theories, and carrying on those dialogues long after the class time ends. It was a rare opportunity for people from different ethnic and racial backgrounds to bond and become allies in the pursuit of knowledge.

The students have often told me how they regularly use terms they learned in my class and have written curriculums for other inmate programs using those terms and theories. Sociology has become a prism through which they can understand their worlds, and provides tools for change that might not have been available to them as uneducated street thugs.

What is also fascinating about the experience is hearing street language being used to explain arcane and deeply theoretical material. The students can translate complex ideas and make them accessible by using words and examples from street or prison life. In one class, a student brought me a key concept sheet of prison lingo. I had provided them with key sociological concepts, and they thought it was only right that I should have a sheet teaching me how to relate to their language. The taught me words like "house," which means someone's cell, "wham whams" and "zoo zoos," which are sweet foods bought from the commissary. A "spread" is a wide range of food that an inmate can legally make in his cell, often with ramen as the base. Then, any and all foods one can find are added to the "spread." Another phrase is "caught my case," which refers to doing a crime and doing time but not taking responsibility for it. Usually, it is similar to "catching" an illness or disease, and thus deflecting responsibility. Finally, a "boneroo" is a nice item in one's possession, like an outfit or a CD player. I must admit that I did not pass the quiz when asked a few weeks later what the terms meant. But I was touched by the effort to educate me.

In a useful analysis of his teaching for Cornell University at Auburn Correctional Facility in New York, Dr. Winthrop Wetherbee saw that no inmate in prison "can avoid the necessity to live a divided existence, to be, in effect, two people" (http://cuauburn.arts,cornell.edu/wetherbee.html). There is the private world—in which the prisoner may be a devout Christian, Jew, or Muslim, or a poet, an adviser to friends and family on the outside—and the public world in the yard, in which survival and posturing is the norm.

Wetherbee saw that it can take years for a prisoner to "achieve a life-saving perspective on this barbarous world, free himself from its grasp, and develop a life of his own." This takes strength, and by being in the classroom, the student has an opportunity to interact with someone who sees him as other than a criminal. When a prisoner is treated as a real human being, a process of feeling better about oneself takes place. By having this dialogue with people who live apart from the insanity of prison, the inmate gains a new perspective that can be a life-saver.

I saw the process that Wetherbee describes, that of life-saving, during the weeks of teaching my course there; I was deeply moved by the efforts made to learn and gain an education. These inmates knew the value of that education, and were not taking it for granted the way many of my young college students did. They avidly read the books, wrote the papers, thought about the ideas, dissected them as individuals and in small groups, and then applied the ideas on a daily basis. Many students hoped to finish their associate's degree and then take classes through the mail to obtain bachelor's degrees. Some knew they would never leave prison but still wanted to better their lives and influence their own children as role models. They also wanted to learn so they could have an effect on other prisoners inside whom they could reach through their knowledge. The moving part for me was watching this process unfold, especially in contrast with students on the outside who did not take their educations seriously at all.

It takes time to build trust with your students inside prison. In the university, your students have had previous success in school and can move ahead with their education and into careers. Many students in prison have not had success in school, and were abandoned by friends and family when they were incarcerated. Building trust is essential. The students need to know that you will come back, and that you do not judge them for what they have done in their pasts. I learned from Wetherbee to "build a relationship of trust—a trust that depends on knowing you will be back week after week, on sensing that you, like them, are feeling your way into the relationship, on seeing you make stupid mistakes." I noticed that eventually, an intimacy occurs in which we as outsiders begin to understand a little "what it is like to be in prison, what it does to a man, and what it teaches him" (http://cuauburn.arts.cornell.edu/wetherbee.html).

One prisoner with whom I developed an excellent rapport was Noel, who was incarcerated for thirty years for a murder committed after he'd been involved in gangs his entire youth. He was given a life sentence, like a thousand other people in California alone who enter prison each year convicted of first- or second-degree murder. There are now over ten thousand of these men who are eligible for release (Mullane, 2012). To date, only 230 have been released on parole in the last twelve years. "Lifers" like Noel, who was sentenced to twenty-five years to life for first-degree murder, are often kept fifteen to twenty years longer than their minimum sentences.

Noel was from Stockton, California, which is notorious for its gang activity and high crime rate. His children and other members of his family remained deeply devoted to him, visiting often and maintaining their strong connections. Noel presented as a gruff, tough-speaking Latino who had taught himself the law and was now volunteering to help others as a jailhouse lawyer. He liked to call himself a "prison litigator." Noel was deeply respected by others in prison because of his knowledge of the law and his dedication to community service and transforming his life inside. Education had become his vehicle for this transformation. His early life had been gang-filled, with migrant parents who traveled around the West. Because he was smart and quick to pick up things, he got into Little League and other sports, winning championships and becoming an outstanding athlete. In fact, in prison, he was on the award-winning San Quentin Giants baseball team.

His story is a painful one. By fourteen, Noel had started fighting and smoking marijuana and PCP. Eventually, he joined a gang and began fighting "everybody and anything." One night when he was out on the streets, his gang decided to rob someone. Noel was eighteen at the time, and when a gun was offered, he stood up and said, "Gimme the gun." As the gang members walked the streets, they encountered two elderly white men, whom they decided to rob. But one of the men tried to grab the gun. As he did, Noel's finger was on the trigger, and he pulled it, killing the old man. Then Noel ran, freaked out by having killed someone who had done nothing to him. Previously, he was comfortable beating other gang members but had never hurt anyone he did not perceive as an enemy. A week later, he was arrested.

By the time I met Noel, he had been inside long enough to have completed his growth from thug to model prisoner. While in jail earlier for a less-violent crime, he had begun looking at religion, at the behest of his mother. At San Quentin, he discovered how tired he was of the life of crime, and began to study and develop a real sense of spirituality. His religion became important to him, and that, along with education, became his tool for change.

The process prisoners go through of awakening, atonement, and transformation was described well by Dr. John Irwin, deceased sociologist from San Francisco State University, in *Lifers: Seeking Redemption in Prison* (Routledge, 2009), and I will describe this evolution in chapter 3. Noel was one of the inmates who served as a bridge for me through the morass of complications and roadblocks encountered when one volunteers in prison. He was released in 2010 after serving just nine days short of thirty years, and has come to lecture in my university class on life in prison and his educational experience. Now married and enrolled in college, he is working as a paralegal for a number of attorneys; his skill as a "prison litigator" has served him well on the outside.

For me, what is equally delightful is to watch the growing self-confidence and self-esteem that occurs as my lifers become more successful as writers and thinkers. Some have never had the experience of competence in the classroom, and this experience helps them realize they have intelligence and skills that are transferable to the world outside, or to interactions in prison. I see many of the men who complete college become role models for others, and a comradeship among students develops. I watch as they begin to mentor each other and help with the material, in addition to acting as writing tutors.

This part of the job brings a fulfillment that makes teaching inside a true joy. Every day, there is a memorable experience, and I am grateful for each one of them every time I am there. As a college professor, I also get to see this kind of growth with my university students, but the process in prison is quicker and seems more profound because of the cold, dark, harsh setting. The students in prison find that their brains become their salvation, unlike college students who have so many other distractions in life. In prison, there are noise and cellblock distractions, there is a constant din that never ends, but the students overcome those to dedicate themselves to their education.

Correctional education is based on the assumption that people can be taught to be law-abiding. It is a shift from the pre-1960s belief system which saw inmates as ill and needing treatment. Instead, the idea took hold in that decade that some people did not have adequate access to legitimate means of reaching status and wealth (McCarty, 2006). Thus, it was believed, if education and programming is provided, people can change through this access to means of upward mobility.

In the '70s, this idea, plus the availability of Pell Grants (named for Rhode Island Democratic Senator Claiborne Pell), made it possible for prisoners to obtain an education through at least 772 college programs available around the country. These federal grants allowed prisons to provide classes offered by accredited institutions of higher education. But although the total budget for prisoners was only .006 percent of all Pell Grants, the tough-on-crime mentality of the late 1980s and early '90s ended the grants' use for prisoner education in 1994 (McCarty, 2006). Lawmakers argued that "free" education for inmates was taking opportunity away from middle- and working-class students who were paying their own way—which was untrue since everyone who applied for a Pell Grant got one, with no limit placed on access. But once the Pell Grants were cut, the percentage of prisoners who were enrolled dropped from 7.3 to 3.8 (McCarty, 2006).

Statistics have shown that it costs more to keep a person in prison for one year than to educate that person by a ratio of 10:1 (www.educationupdate.com). Prison education programs have been found to have a significant impact on recidivism rates. The exact effect is difficult to quantify because the rates differ in various studies, but all of them show that reincarceration is diminished and that education promotes successful reentry into society.

According to the U.S. Bureau of Justice Statistics, 95 percent of all prisoners eventually will be released. As we know, most of them are young members of groups with low income and low educational attainment. Without an education, more than half return to prison in three years. In addition to reducing the likelihood of this return, education programs give the students an opportunity to lead healthy, productive, and meaningful lives both inside and outside the prison. Higher education helps build communities of learning within individual prisons that support intellectual and personal growth to equip students to lead economically and socially stable lives upon release.

One longitudinal research project found that of 3,200 prisoners studied, reincarceration for those with some education was 21 percent while those with less education had a 31 percent rate. The drop in recidivism is large and has important fiscal and policy implications. The authors believed that education provided a real payoff to the public in terms of crime reduction and improved employment of ex-offenders (Steurer, Smith, and Tracy, 2001).

Another study found that recidivism rates were as low as 55 percent for those who had attended some college while in prison (McCarty, 2006). Even though there is no federal funding for such programs, the American Council on Education has found that the number of prisoner education settings is rising again (www.acenet). In 2005, the Institute for Higher Education Policy found that there were only thirty programs in 2001-2 and forty-three in 2003-4. Fifteen state correctional systems accounted for 89 percent of all incarcerated students enrolled in such programs. Texas, North Carolina, and the Federal Bureau of Prisons have more than 10 percent of the total prison population enrolled in higher education.

In North Carolina, a partnership between the Department of Corrections and the Community College System offers classes to almost one-third of the entire prison population each year. In California, similar partnerships are being developed between community colleges and the Department of Corrections and Rehabilitation, using mostly online courses rather than the face-to-face method offered at San Quentin. Part of the appeal of the San Quentin program is the individualized mentorship and tutoring students receive from other prisoners as well as from professors and teaching assistants at Bay Area colleges, which ensures a greater completion rate.

Any prison education program must have a strong partnership with a university. Without that commitment at the very top, the programs often suffer or are not sustaining. The program I established at Elmira Correctional Facility with Ithaca College languished when the college's top administration withdrew its support, eventually shutting it down. The program at San Quentin has thrived because of the educational partnership with Patten University and the Prison University Project. Boston University founded a prison education program in 1972 that has graduated 160 B.A. students and fifty master's students as a result of the university's commitment to educate prisoners. The students receive tuition, texts, and supplies. Where an institution of higher education makes this commitment, the programs have survived even without financial assistance from the government. The universities realize that this is an investment in the future of our youth, and serves an important social justice function for our society. It is admirable that they have made such a commitment.

My experience teaching in prison has actually informed and changed the way I teach outside the prison. I find myself covering the issues of the criminal justice system and the mass incarceration crisis more in my university classes with undergraduate students. I bring in former prisoners to educate them, I assign books about prison, and I bring groups of students to prison on a regular basis so they can see first-hand all that I am teaching them. I also bring a correctional officer to my class so the students can hear all sides of the debate on incarceration, and I make sure there are exercises on the issue in class so the students can understand how people become criminals and how we treat them in our system. I watch students open their eyes and hearts in a way that is truly moving to me as an educator. Transformations take place as these college students grapple with the stereotypes they have learned from the mass media, and see how the stereotypes about prisoners are not always true.

As a college professor and scholar, I have often felt trapped in an ivory tower, one not grounded in the real world. By teaching in prison, I am forced to experience the most painful of human institutions. I have deepened my knowledge, found myself more forgiving and understanding of human frailties, and seen the ugly consequences of social inequality and society's unequal opportunity structures. For these reasons and others, I find it a privilege to work with prisoners.

Perhaps the most significant outcome for me of teaching in the prison's college program was my own growing sense of doing something meaningful for society. I have encountered colleagues who are amazed that I would want to do such a thing, wondering why a person would ever want to work with convicted felons. I marvel at those who do not understand, since they have failed to perceive the value of every human being and see the potential for redemption in everyone. Other people ask me how they can participate, because they see the value of such work. I resonate with those who want to know more and to join me in this invaluable experience.

Chapter 3

Prisoners Are People, Too:
Self-Help Groups and New Leaf on Life

Soon after finishing my class at San Quentin in 2004, a student contacted me to ask if I would sponsor a prisoner-initiated and -run self-help group called New Leaf on Life lifers' group. I was honored to be asked. When I found out that the group would meet monthly, it suited me and my schedule better than a weekly class. The group's purpose, as stated in its fact sheet, is based on the belief that a lifer who is serious about changing for the better, and is then provided with a proper setting, information, and resources, can become an asset to his community. The group was initially run by three prisoners who were self-selected as founders and leaders.

San Quentin is remarkable in its numerous self-help groups that are prisoner-initiated and prisoner-run. Because the prison is in the Bay Area, quite a few socially concerned citizens volunteer with these programs. It is actually impossible to identify them all, but one of the most visible is the ARC, a sixteen-week addiction recovery and counseling program that includes psychoeducation classes and is staffed by professionally trained inmate peer counselors.

Other programs include IMPACT, which stands for Incarcerated Men Putting Away Childish Things and works to reform the character of men who want to become responsible and mature, and Keeping It Real, a group that teaches life skills and peer education on women's perspectives, fear of success, healing the wounded father-son relationship, and other topics of interest to the organizers (Irwin, 2009).

Courses in nonviolent communication use role playing to teach conflict avoidance, listening skills, cooperative learning, and bridging cultural differences, among other subjects. SQUIRES (San Quentin Utilization of Inmate Resources, Experiences and Studies) brings juveniles to the prison for a program akin to "Scared Straight." San Quentin TRUST (Teaching Responsibility Utilizing Training for the Development of Incarcerated Men) has a set of programmed sessions using sociological concepts to help prisoners with issues of self-growth, and the Victim Offender Reconciliation Group (VORG) brings rape victims together with prisoners for discussion and reconciliation (Irwin, 2009).

In addition, there are programs like A.A. and N.A., a Vietnam Veterans group, religious groups of all denominations, Native American sweat lodges, food sales, and health fairs. Countless prisoners avail themselves of these groups, and men sometimes are seen running from program to program as if driven by the hope of developing self-awareness and bettering themselves. All this programming is done in conjunction with the full-time jobs held by all mainline prisoners. Life is busy for everyone in this hub of activity. Sometimes, a prisoner has worked all day, taken a class, showered, and then runs over to a self-help group to continue his education.

When I first attended the New Leaf group, the specifics of what we would do were unclear. I was joined as a sponsor by John Kelly, a retired priest and school principal who had been volunteering at San Quentin for years in a Catholic organization called Kairos. John is well loved by the men at SQ, and it is a pleasure to work with him because of his humor, life experience, and intelligence.

At the first session, I suggested that perhaps I could bring in college professors from Sonoma State to lecture on topics of interest to the men. I thought it would be much like what I had done at Elmira Correctional Facility. John and I assumed this pattern would run its course and that eventually, a new format might evolve. However, after six years, the format remains the same. Once a month, John or I bring a professor or public speaker who is chosen to either educate the inmates on subjects they want to learn about, or discuss subjects that would help them with parole and enhancing their self-awareness.

The variety of topics has been far-reaching and provocative. One month, I might ask a philosophy professor to speak on the meaning of life, and the next month, I might bring a law professor who teaches how to write a habeas corpus petition for the courts. The subjects are chosen by the prisoners; I ask them what they are interested in, then find a speaker for that topic. The list of subjects they have chosen includes, "how to be a better person," psychologists talking about "lack of insight," tools for dealing with anger, the state's three-strikes policy which imposes a life sentence on anyone convicted of three felonies, triggers to responding to difficult situations, public speaking skills, reentry issues, and meeting a victim rights activist. We try to meet all the requests.

Although two of the founders have been transferred to other prisons, continued leadership is provided by the third, Don Baylor, a sixty-one-year-old African-American from Richmond,

California, who has already served twenty years for murder. Baylor, the group's chairperson, is well organized, regularly sending out notices about the meetings, arranging for the forms called "chronos" which prove that the men attended, and providing the certificates we give after a year of participation. He also sets up the fund-raising food sales that are an enormous amount of work to implement.

Don meets us, cane in hand, as we cross the yard, and welcomes the speakers, students, and myself as we arrive. He is so helpful in orienting the guests to the subcultures of the institution and making them feel welcome. Don humanizes the place, educating the speakers as to what they are seeing, all done with charm and humor.

Thirty-five regulars attend the sessions. Some members of the group have been paroled or transferred to other facilities. All the men are lifers. Over the years, a few stand out because of their charisma and personalities. Phylo is a Jewish African-American in his fifties who has been incarcerated for almost thirty years. He transferred to San Quentin about five years ago, and came with a chip on his shoulder, often finding himself in difficulties with the other prisoners. In fact, Don wanted to throw him out of the group because he was seen as noncooperative. I suggested that we give him another chance, and the results have been remarkable.

One hot summer day, most group members were on lockdown and not allowed to leave their cellblocks or come to the programming. Somehow, I had been allowed in with one of my law professor speakers. Phylo found us a spot at a dugout of the Giants ballpark, where the group met. He also ran around to gather all the members who could make it, and we held our session in the bright, hot sunlight. It would not have happened without Phylo.

This was a guy who had a difficult childhood and has many years more to serve. In a personal essay, he spoke of being a "victim of the socioeconomic circumstances of American society." The poverty and low standard of education that he received created "a mental pathology" in him. As a juvenile delinquent, he was affected by a host of addictions, especially abuse of cocaine which led him to lose his "mental faculties." In 1983, he was arrested for kidnapping and burglary and received two consecutive life terms with the possibility of parole."

In prison, he has spent most of his time reading and learning. As he says, "I owe my life and good health. If not for the help of seasoned professors and educated volunteers, I would still be steaming and drowning in a sea of ignorance." Instead, Phylo received his associate's degree in 2008 and continues to accumulate college credits.

Most rewarding, he says, are the self-help groups "which allow the individual to experience some spiritual awakening and growth." He goes on to say, "Like leaves falling to the ground only to reenter the cycle of life and death, I am now a 'new leaf' who is ready to provide clean oxygen for all of life's creatures."

Phylo says, very movingly, that "for a quarter of a century, I failed to accomplish anything meaningful in my life." He entered the prison doors at the age of twenty-seven, and for the past twenty-eight years, he has positioned himself in a "place of opportunity and change." He sees himself as "now a partner in the business of creation—building up and not tearing down. There can be no better way to live in the world than to be of service of creation. Peace and happiness can only be measured by the strides we make and the quality of life we make for our own humanity and for others."

Another inmate with whom I have had many conversations is Jinryu, a white man from Brooklyn, N.Y., who was raised in a middle-class family, attended college, and became a sergeant in the Marine Corps. He was also married and had a child. Unfortunately, he was abusing drugs and alcohol when he was in the military, and while high on PCP one Christmas time, he needed money and decided to rob a liquor store. He took a military revolver, and when he panicked after robbing the store, he kidnapped a man, put him in a car, and drove away. Later, he had the man lie on the ground, and when the captive moved, Jinryu, who was high, shot him five times. The victim was permanently disabled. Jinryu has served over thirty years and been denied parole at all his hearings.

Jinryu is a Buddhist who meditates early every morning to avoid the noise and din that fills the cellblock tiers when the other men wake. John Irwin quotes him as saying:

"So I really started looking at the things that I do in my whole life. If I can't be at peace with myself, how can I ever expect to be at peace with other people around me? And so then I began this long and processed self-reflection. Watching what I do, whenever I do—and at first, fortunately, it became a very egotistical thing. I thought that, Oh, it's so great I can create this wall around [my crime] and be protected by all this negativity, but the problem is just the sitting in the eye of this hurricane of a storm, and so I had to really learn it was about me opening up and just being more open. And so I just started slowly working on who I was, and I did it through meditation" (Irwin, 2009, p 94).

Jinryu's meditation helped him realize that he had caused pain in another person's life. He had been on the run for six years with his wife and daughter, and watching his girl grow up helped him realize that his own humanity was dead. His daughter helped him reawaken, and when he was finally arrested and incarcerated, his cellmate introduced him to Buddhism. He did not really begin his practice until five years later, as a way to rise above the fray that surrounded him in prison. After coming to San Quentin, he wrote to a Buddhist peace fellowship and asked its members to help start the San Quentin Buddhadharma Sangha. As a result, a group of like-minded men found a safe and peaceful place to practice (Nahmias, 2009).

As you might be able to tell, the lifers group is filled with men of depth and substance. They may have committed grave and terrible crimes. But they are not grave and terrible people. In my group, I have learned what I teach, which is that "prisoners are people, too." I find that the discussions are often deep and thoughtful. There are no superficial references to popular culture; instead, the discussions are about troubling and substantial issues. Not long ago, I brought in two scholars on the nonviolent social movements that have happened in places like Libya, Yemen, and Burma. The guys had read about these places, asked deep questions, and knew what was going on in all the settings we talked about.

One of the faculty members who led the discussion, Dr. Cynthia Boaz, was impressed with the whole class, and said that she felt an "oppressive sense of anxiety and sadness embrace me." It was the buildings and grounds that had struck her. "Especially after seeing a cellblock," she said, "it is hard to imagine how any person can spend a significant amount of time in a prison like San Quentin and still retain their sense of humanity." To Boaz, "it was obvious that the physical design of the place is intended to create a sense of smallness, of intimidation, of dehumanization."

Her observations were that "there is no illusion whatsoever of liberty; the place is created to remind the prisoner that—at least while he carries the status of active inmate—he is under another's control." To her way of thinking, a prisoner "sleeps, eats, works, and even socializes on someone else's calendar. Of course, that is the point, and as such, it's made very effectively."

But she asks, "What of the people who live in this system for years, sometimes decades, on end?" Boaz and her mentor and colleague, Michael Nagler, offered a short course on Nonviolence and Nonviolent Action, a subject she had introduced to thousands of students over six years. What struck her about the inmates at San Quentin was "how open they were to the material."

There is often a deconstruction phase that most of her students go through to effectively integrate knowledge about nonviolence, because the material runs so counter to the conventional wisdom on concepts such as power, conflict, and violence. "But this phase was not necessary for the guys in the New Leaf program," Boaz says. "They 'got it' immediately."

She wondered why. Her first instinct was to give credit to the subject—"by definition, it is empowering and rehumanizing and inspirational." She noted that "nonviolence is all about actively promoting life." But upon deeper reflection, she realized "that an equal amount of—if not more—credit should go to the men of New Leaf on Life, who have found a way to not only retain their humanity but who have discovered an earnest desire to be better people."

She felt "that during the course of the class, I kept forgetting I was in a room full of prison inmates," and remembers "one man whose face I will never forget. It was sweet and kind and thoughtful. He is about fifty-five, and has been in San Quentin for thirty-eight years. He had a twinkle in his eye when he spoke about his next parole hearing—scheduled for summer 2012. All he wants, he told me, is to meet and hug his ten grandchildren."

Boaz didn't know what the man's crime was, but she did know that "when he committed it, he was very young." And she knew that the "person I saw sitting at the table listening to me and Michael speak about nonviolence had not a bitter bone in his body. It was a striking lesson for me, both personally and professionally." She was so moved to think that "if this person who has spent nearly four decades deprived of his personal freedom and dignity can find the silver lining in his life, then who are we to not?" Finally she said that "if he and others like him can find a way to want to continue to learn, love, and forgive (themselves and others), then shouldn't we who live our lives with the full blessings of liberty every day do so as well?" She had "gratitude for meeting the men at the San Quentin New Leaf on Life program because they remind me to never, ever take my own life circumstances for granted and to always try to live by the principles of the subject I teach—nonviolence."

Other faculty members who have attended have been equally moved and educated by interacting with the prisoners. Dr. Eric Williams, a criminologist, had been to many prisons around the country and had lectured on his research but had never put the prisoners he saw and his research together. He felt that talking "to inmates about my research on prison towns felt a little odd, since my research has mainly focused on prison employees and administrators." But he found that the guys were as attentive as any class he had ever taught, and asked really solid questions, "often seeing things from a different perspective than the academic audiences" he usually speaks to.

The discussion that developed about Brown v. Plata, the California prison overcrowding case decided by the U.S. Supreme Court, showed him that the students' knowledge of it far exceeded his own, with good reason. "But what amazed me was their reaction to who was going to be released under the court order. They knew that in terms of recidivism, guys like them were much better bets than the people who were likely to be released," since drug offenders and other lower-level inmates actually have a much higher recidivism rate than murderers.

While Williams tried to answer their questions, he realized that "despite being stepped on in so many ways in life, these guys did not seem to want to accept that something as crass as politics could stop the government from doing the smart thing and letting some of them out." He found that the prisoners "were amazed that the decision was not going to be made based on what made the most sense from a fairness and public safety standpoint but based on what kept the politicians most protected from their constituents. For some reason, that reaction is what has stuck with me most. I found the hopefulness of it both heartwarming and heartbreaking at the same time."

Another professor, this one of history, spoke about race in her talk at San Quentin. Dr. Amy Kittelstrom was warmly received by the guys of New Leaf in May 2008. "Cliches like 'tragic waste of human potential' came to life for me in a place where so many men so fundamentally like my Sonoma State students are stored," she said, "without whitewashing the seriousness of their crimes and how violence and lawlessness distinguish them from my regular students."

Kittelstrom found that the main difference between the prisoners and her outside students seemed to be that "my students are working toward a better future for themselves and hence better for society, while these men could see no future different from their present but wanted one just as much, had energy and insights that could add value to a society from which they are instead literally walled off." Penetrating that boundary through New Leaf on Life meant that "I can bring into my future teaching an increment of their experience, and although I hope the prisoners gained something from the material I presented and the discussion I fostered, my only certain knowledge is that they educated me."

For example, on the topic of self-segregation by race, she saw "one of the most stark facts of San Quentin" in California's at-

tempt that spring to enforce desegregation in the cells. Her theory
that living together as inmates do would emphasize their common
humanity to people from different backgrounds was "tested by
their practice of life *in extremis*," Kittelstrom said, and she came
away believing that those who are "affected by policies, even the
unfree, should have a voice in the formulation of those policies."
In the end, her experience at San Quentin convinced her that
"the separation of what the progressive activist Jane Addams called
'the social classes' is poisonous to democracy, and that more com-
merce between those of different backgrounds and prospects
means more understanding for everyone—that, in Addams's
words, 'the social relation is essentially a reciprocal relation.' "

Dr. Lynn Cominsky, a physicist who spoke on the black holes
of the universe, was struck by the prisoners' social isolation. She
had never given an astronomy talk without showing PowerPoint
slides, which are not allowed in the prison. She knew it would
be a challenge, and had some trepidation as well about her "personal safety, technical competence," including worry that she
would not be able to connect with people so far removed from
her "typical public audiences of amateur astronomers, college
students, or at least the scientifically literate public."

Cominsky chose a very simple topic—"Seeing the Invisible"—
to show the lifers that there was more to the universe than what
their eyes could see. But many of the examples that she typically
uses to "illustrate different types of radiation—such as microwave
ovens and remote control devices—were not things to which these
folks have been exposed." She found that most of them had been
incarcerated since before those things were invented.

"This was quite an eye-opener for me, as I am a true
technophile, and, of course, never considered the fact that common electronics would be beyond their life experiences." But
what she saw was that "despite these glitches in my understand-

ing of their experiences, the audience seemed very interested, were unfailingly polite and respectful, and I felt that I really was able to open their eyes somewhat to the universe around them, even if they can't see much of it."

Another social psychologist who spoke to the group was struck by the "ordinariness of the prisoners." Dr. Diana Grant, an expert in criminology, said she had wondered whether they would really want to hear her talk about research on jurors and eyewitnesses. But she found that "I need not have worried. They were some of the most attentive listeners I have had, and several asked thoughtful questions or gave responsive answers when I threw out some questions and asked for feedback."

But what Grant most took away from the experience was "reaffirmation of my sense of the very ordinariness of these men." She knew that they all had been sentenced to life in prison for murder, and that few would ever earn parole. She said she had "always endeavored to communicate to my students in the free world that there is not such a bright line distinction between such folks (inmates) and the rest of us—an idea that some students reject out of hand."

Her view, she knew, "does not mean that we accept killing as somehow inevitable, but it does demand that we acknowledge the voluminous evidence supporting the hypothesis that people who kill others are not necessarily monsters or anomalous outliers." She was surprised when a young inmate told her during a break in the SQ class that "he was not going to deny that he had killed another man, and described how a road-rage incident involving the driver of the car he was riding in and another car turned into a fight, and within a few minutes, he had stabbed and killed one of the passengers from the other car."

What struck Grant was that "this man is paying his dues for taking the life of another person, by being sentenced to life imprisonment." But she also asked herself, "Could I truly say that I myself would never do something that resulted in the death of another?" Her conversation with the young man had reminded her "that the distinction between inmates and the rest of us is to such a large degree a socially constructed myth, a comforting belief presented to the public in order to rationalize our massive prison system." Grant knew the point is "that many, many people who have killed other people are not just like us—they are us."

Another conversation she had with an older inmate helped her look at the social explanations for crime. "As we were both walking with our canes down a steep path to the portable building that was our destination, he began talking about why people come to San Quentin. These young ones, he said, 'you can't talk about rehabilitatin' them, 'cause they've never been *habilitated* in the first place.'" She heard his voice underlining the word "habilitated" and asked what he meant.

He went on to say that many of the older inmates had ended up in prison because even though they were raised with "good morals" in a good family and knew right from wrong, they had made a bad mistake and taken a life. But in his view, many of the younger inmates came from an environment where they never had a chance to learn right from wrong—addicted parents, violence all around them—so you couldn't talk about getting them rehabilitated because they were never "habilitated" in the first place. What chance did they have to learn the right way to act when they grew up surrounded by violence?

Grant recounts this conversation and the old man's point to her students when they discuss the etiology of crime. "What do you think of this idea? I ask my students. What are the implications for crime prevention? What does this mean for our attempts to help inmates become rehabilitated? This usually leads to a very thought-provoking discussion."

When Dr. Rick Luttman, a long-time professor of mathematics who also teaches in the Prison University Project, spoke to the lifers, he was struck by their desire to become productive and contributing members of society. He talked with them about the Eskimos' ways of dealing with conflict resolution nonviolently, and explained that his partner is Eskimo and that he has lived in Alaska off and on since 1967, including much time in a native village—hence his expertise on the subject.

"I found the students very attentive and willing to get involved in the conversation through questions and comments as I went along," he said. Long after the talk, many students approached him on his regular visits to San Quentin and told him how valuable that lecture was. "This is exactly what I was hoping to hear," Luttman said. "I chose the topic because I thought it might be directly relevant to their own past or present experiences." Some prisoners told him he had helped them personally to deal with "their own impulses to violence, and some have even been inspired to join groups dedicated to preventing or reducing violence in the prison environment."

Luttman said he finds his talks to the San Quentin audience very fulfilling. "Of course, I speak only to a relatively small percentage of the inmate population who have self-selected to come hear me," he said. But he finds, as have other professors, that the students "are among the most highly motivated, dedicated, and receptive that I have had in my entire teaching career, which now spans almost half a century."

Like other professors, he is touched by the fact that "education, for these men, is a very serious matter—not just something you do because college is the next thing that comes after high school, and mom and dad are paying for it, and there are some great parties." He adds that the inmates "recognize that they need to make themselves into functioning, productive citizens if they ever expect to stay out of prison once released, and that making up deficiencies in their education is a major step."

In addition to working with New Leaf on Life and taking college professors and lawyers to address the group, I have also taken a number of student groups into the prison to meet the lifers and be educated about prison life and what incarceration does to people. The group that is the most effective for reaching students is TRUST, a self-help group that runs weekly workshops for prisoners for seven months. Its mission statement describes its goal as to "educate, organize, and lead ourselves into becoming a vibrant force inspiring change in our community and understanding and reawakening of our histories, cultures, and values." The group works with modules on topics needed to change and grow such as how to be a leader, developing a self-respectful value system, and dealing with family.

My experience taking students in to meet with the leaders of TRUST has been remarkable. I believe the students' words speak for themselves. One of them, Heather Coyne, spoke of arriving at SQ with "the conceived notion that all prisoners were serial killers and would continue to murder people upon their parole." But the members of TRUST she talked with remolded her view completely.

"First, I was shocked by how remorseful the inmates were about their crimes, which most had committed before age eighteen." She also discovered that most of them were convicted as adults, even though they were teenagers, because of the premeditation or sophistication of their crimes.

Second, she began to understand "how the social construction around them leads them to become criminals." As an example, "one inmate, Charlie, stated that he did not have consequences growing up. Since his father was out of his life, his mother had to work during the day and did not have the ability to monitor Charlie." Heather learned that if Charlie did not go to school or do his homework, there were no repercussions because his mother was not around to be involved.

"Third, most of the inmates did not have a father figure in their lives, or if there was one, he was physically abusing the mother in the family." She heard the case of David, who said he had no incentive to do well in school or succeed in life. His mother loved him but was not an authoritative figure, so David started hanging around with the wrong crowd. Heather found that some of the prisoners' histories were of "aggressive behavior problems, some had hostile, inept, or neglectful parents, and others grew up with a loving mother and had no past delinquencies." She learned that the "main risk factors for these youth (to progress to criminals) are poor parenting and affiliation with antisocial/troubled peers, the second usually the result of the first."

After her visit, she felt empathetic toward the inmates because she understood the circumstances of their upbringing that had led them to San Quentin. "They were not aware of the consequences, did not think how the violent act would impact their future, and the only role models in their lives were criminals. How could they not go down that path?"

Heather learned that "initially, the inmates were socialized to become delinquents (through lack of parental control), and subsequently, their brain had not fully matured when the acts of violence were committed." She also learned that "this is pivotal because in adolescence, the prefrontal cortex has not finished developing, the part of the brain that is responsible for planning, thinking ahead, weighing risks, and impulse control."

Furthermore, Heather became most interested in the events that had led to the imprisonment of these people, whom she now considers "my friends." By peeling off the layers of the onion, she grew to understand the circumstances of childhood that had brought them to SQ. "I was able to apply sociology definitions such as blaming the victim, self-fulfilling prophesy, and strain theory. From visiting San Quentin and talking to the members of the TRUST, my perception of prisoners has changed. (Inmates have rehabilitated themselves.)" She became motivated to help them reach parole. "I remember the words from Elaine Leeder," Heather says. "Prisoners are people, too."

Another student was far more detailed in an essay she wrote describing her experiences at San Quentin. Taylor Dickinson's analysis had a level of sophistication and specificity that was remarkable. She saw "the dehumanization that started the instant we walked into the first building for the second security check of the day." As she entered, she saw that "it was a small, bleak area with metal bars acting as dividing walls. We signed in, were scanned with a handheld metal detector, and stamped with an invisible ink. If you didn't have that stamp on the way out, you weren't leaving."

Taylor was appalled as "the next step was to crowd all twenty-four of us into a small area that was supposed to be only for ten—a cage, if you will—that had doors controlled by a guard behind a thick wall of glass in an area that set them higher than us. We all had to hold up our IDs before they could push the button to open the second door, filing us out into the courtyard of the prison."

As we walked to another guard station, she saw that "two men in all denim were standing waiting to greet us. It took a moment to realize these men were prisoners, and there was a reason we weren't allowed to wear denim on this trip."

Taylor went on: "The first man, the only one of the two who addressed us at first, introduced himself as Red, and he would be escorting us to the room where the other men were waiting. While he spoke, we were all huddled fairly close together."

Taylor goes on to tell what happened then: " 'Hey! Stay away from drugs!' someone cackled out a small open window right above the words 'Adjustment Center' painted on the building. Those who heard giggled with nervousness. The Adjustment Center was where the more 'troublesome' prisoners were kept. Yes sir," Taylor said in her essay, "if that was where drugs get you, I have even more motive to stay away from them."

Taylor continued: "As we entered the yard, a few men called out to us, but I could not process what they were saying. I was too uneasy." She was surprised when "Red turned to face us as he walked backward, an easy smile on his face as he asked, 'Are you guys nervous?' We giggled and looked around to see each other's reactions."

The group was taken to a portable room like those you see outside school buildings, with a chain link fence around it. Taylor went on: "In the room, two men were handing out the San Quentin News. The two or three men there were dressed in white T-shirts and jeans, one wearing a white baseball cap waving at us. He introduced himself as Charlie as we took our seats, most of us sticking together."

Red was in charge for the day, getting the group settled and starting the introductions around the circle. "He told us his name, his real name, and a little about himself," Taylor said. "The rest of us said just our names, and the big circle [finished the introductions] in about thirty seconds." Red called it "the fastest circle I've ever seen!"

Taylor described the men in white T-shirts and jeans as the "pillars" in the prison community, the good ones to look up to. "The nerves quickly began to fade away," she said, "and by the time Professor Leeder stopped the discussion and made the men mix in with us in the circle, it wasn't as scary as I thought it would be." Then, Taylor went on, "The oldest member in the room, a man they called Doc, switched seats with Vinny and sat down next to me." She shook his soft hand as he introduced himself to her as Larry, "but the boys here call me Doc." She smiled and told him her name. "I wasn't afraid at all to be in his grasp. From then on, the men sitting between us all suddenly began to seem like real people."

Taylor saw that they were educated, understanding, funny, and all had their own defined personalities. "It's impossible to truly know someone in a few hours, but they did their best," she said. "Personal stories were shared, both from the incarcerated and the free, and I found that I was able to relate to some of the stories or emotions they described." She learned that prison life isn't like "Lockup" or other TV shows. "The way the media warps these ideas is disturbing because it's all just playing into the stereotypes that they (the media) already created in our heads and showing us what we want to see."

Taylor said that one of the biggest ideas she took from the experience was separating the crime from the person. She felt no doubt that many of the men regret what they did. Most of them were very young when they committed their crimes. Most were in for murder, some gang-related, some committed under the influence of drugs and/or alcohol. One of the prisoners had been in the system since he was sixteen for being with a person who shot someone.

"Yes, these are bad things," Taylor said. "But you realize quickly from these stories that these guys aren't much different from anyone else; they just happened to take one or two more wrong turns in their lives, and that landed them in prison—most already in for half of their lives or more."

She learned that crimes hurt not only the victims and their families but also can affect those who committed the crimes and their families for even longer. "I'm not saying this to justify the crime," Taylor said, "but as one man described, 'It was just one instant that ruined the rest of my life.' "

At one point, she was deeply moved as Charlie described how he had been shackled for days while a court decided whether he could be sent to an adult institution at the age of sixteen. "The pain and loneliness he described was heartbreaking, the need for someone, something, anything to be there for him." Taylor cried as he said, "I didn't care if it was a person or a cockroach running across the floor. I needed something." As he talked, the pain was visible to her, and she felt sick that such a carefree, amusing guy could be put through something so horrible.

She said she believed that everyone who meets the men of TRUST will gain a new perspective on the prison system or our entire society. "Social change is what the world could use right now," she said, "and we've seen from the past that it isn't a very easy thing to make happen. I'm not trying to preach to anyone, just like the men weren't trying to preach to us. I just want those who did not have the experience to be informed to the best of my ability."

Taylor said afterward that she wished everyone could have an experience like hers with the TRUST members so they "could see exactly what it's like to have stereotypes broken and see someone transform right before your eyes simply by listening to what they had to say." The TRUST motto of "building a bridge from the inside out" is exactly what happened to her that cold Saturday morning.

Her final words described Red walking the group back to the courtyard where he had met them, and everyone saying goodbye there. She told of going back through the cage, ten at a time as they were supposed to, and then having their invisible stamps checked. There were no problems, she notes, and suddenly, "the surreal experience was over. No one was mugged, no one was hurt, no one was even looked at the wrong way. We were never going to have a chance to be in San Quentin again—at least not the same way. We were back to civilization where, unlike the men inside, we were free to go."

Finally, another student, Claire Keegan, wrote this powerful essay. "My favorite piece of literature," she said, "is Dr. Seuss's children's book *Horton Hears a Who*. As a child, the line 'A person's a person, no matter how small' resonated with me because I thought to myself, 'Hey, I might be a little kid, but I am a person just like everyone else. Why am I not treated equally?' " Then as she grew up, her thoughts on this phrase grew to include women and others who are discriminated against. "If a person is a person, then why am I treated lesser for being a female? Why are people judged based on ethnicity or socioeconomic status?"

But although she believed that people are people regardless of their gender, race, or income, "I still had a negative viewpoint on prisoners," she said, "because the ones I knew personally, and the ones portrayed in the media, are the lowest of the low and are people who are either incapable, or choose not to change for the better while they are in prison." She accepted the stereotype that all prisoners were behind bars for a good reason and should not be allowed out because they were not going to be productive members of society.

On her trip to San Quentin, she wrote, "I was fortunate to meet men, not prisoners or convicted felons but genuine men. My expectations based on stereotypes had been challenged when I met this group of men." She had expected angry, hard prisoners who wanted nothing but to serve their time and get back as soon as possible to the lives they had always known: drugs, violence, and perpetual hardships. She was pleasantly surprised "to meet such a fine group of men who were honest, respectful, and real."

When she heard them talk, she was shocked at their wide vocabulary and the educated way they spoke to the group. "These men seemed more like college-level professors than convicted felons serving a life sentence," she said, and thought to herself, "No way. These men could not have committed the atrocious crimes they were convicted of. She discovered that the men she met were no longer the criminals they had been when they were first incarcerated.

"These men have taken the painful journey of looking inside themselves and changing what needed to be changed," Claire said. "They were no longer the angry and confused victims of society." She saw that they had taken the time to really look at their lives, their choices, and themselves, and were working hard every day to become the strong, honorable, and respected men they are now.

"They treated me with more kindness, understanding, and respect than any other men I have ever encountered," she said. She saw that their "crimes may have been tragic, but they have used their time in prison to their advantage and I feel that now, these men are even better people than many law-abiding citizens I know outside of prison." She said she hoped to one day see the men she had met released from incarceration because she knew that "they have changed for the better, and they want nothing more than to help change our society so that other young men and women do not have to follow the path that they regrettably chose."

Claire ended her essay by saying, "A person is a person, no matter their past. Everyone makes mistakes in life, some minor, some grave, but what we chose to do after personal failure should be what defines us, not the error in judgment." She said she also saw that "prisoners are people too, and as a society, we have failed to give these human beings the necessary tools to change their lives for the better. Stripping ex-convicts of their natural-born rights is not the answer." She added that, "All prisons need to have the rehabilitation programs and community support that the men I met had to turn prisoners and convicted felons into respectable men with a prosperous future."

My experience in prison has also brought me in touch with elements of my own heritage. Because I am Jewish, I was amazed to find Jews in prison, and was drawn to attending services on the inside when invited. I wanted to know about these people who shared my value system and yet had committed violent crimes; it seemed incomprehensible to me. Those of us who are Jewish find it hard to imagine other Jews who have committed violent crimes, and to find Jewish people in prison serving long sentences. It is often unbelievable to us that Jews have broken the strong moral code that pervades our culture and religion.

Since this is "my life with lifers," I found my way to this subgroup. And what I found is the undeniable reality that there are Jews inside—although only about one tenth of one percent, 1,700 out of the U.S. prison population of 1.6 million. (Additionally, ten of the country's prisoners on death row are Jewish.)

Nonetheless, Jews have been criminals since they began immigrating to the U.S., with the most notable being Meyer Lansky, one of the most long-lived and most powerful of all. There was also Bugsy Siegel, Dutch Schultz, and Gyp the Blood, to name just a few. The Jewish gangster has long been a historical fact and one that has captured the imagination of the public.

It is often feared in the Jewish community that a few "bad Jews" will give other Jews a bad name. That is true today with the arrest and conviction of Bernie Madoff for his Ponzi scheme which bilked thousands, including Elie Wiesel, of their savings. There is fear that the crimes will set off a wave of anti-Semitism and anti-Jewish rhetoric like what is rampant in parts of Europe, and which many believe lies just below the surface of American society.

Jews in prison face difficulties, as do all prisoners. But participation in religion is encouraged inside, with the opportunity to get kosher meals and observe the Sabbath and holidays. A Jewish chaplain usually is available, and prisoners are encouraged to attend services and follow the religious proscriptions. Prison officials believe that engaging in religious practices makes for a less violent or angry person with whom to work.

In addition to services for Catholic, Protestant, Muslim, and Native American prisoners, there is a church at San Quentin for those who identify as Wiccan. Since the Jewish chapel is shared with the Muslim group, a schedule has been established to avoid overlapping or conflicting use. It is smaller than the Protestant and Catholic chapels, and no signs or symbols are left out after the services.

Probably some of the most noteworthy Jewish events I have experienced were a bar mitzvah of two congregants and two Passover services. The bar mitzvah was a moving and significant event for which Yohannan and Bruce rehearsed many months. Yohannan, who was recently paroled, was extremely repentant and had found his way back to Judaism while incarcerated. With his *yarmulke* and fringed prayer *tzitzit*, he was an odd sight on the yard. But he never had an infraction on his record while in prison, and was a model citizen. Because he had not been bar mitzvahed as a young man, he chose to do it now.

He had been born in Los Angeles in 1957, the fourth of six children born to Jewish parents, his father from the Bronx, N.Y., and mother from Rochester, N.Y. Other than his own experience, Yohannan knew very little about his father. His parents had met after World War II, come to Los Angeles around 1950, and married.

His earliest memory is being punched in the face at the age of three; he knew it was his father. Getting hit was something he would become accustomed to. What he never got used to was the emotional abuse. The words hurt him most, that and being in constant fear—or terror is a better word—of being hit or kicked. It was worse than actually getting hit: "Have you ever had a bully throw a punch at you and stop just inches before your face, and then recoil and thrust their fist at you over and over again, and each time the fear of getting hit was too much to bear?"

So Yohannan acted out just to get it over with. One thing his father could not tolerate was his stuttering. "My first words were stutters, so I stuttered just to get hit and get it over with. My father also called me a dummy or an idiot or stupid when I couldn't communicate." So he was never good enough; no matter how hard he worked or what his talents were, he was forever just an idiot. "I played the drums and sang. I painted and drew. I loved animals. I had a black cat I named George. I loved the outdoors and nature, and most of all, I loved to pray."

In his elementary school years, he lived in La Puente, California. There was no synagogue in the area, but a rabbi lived around the block in a house Yohannan would walk to for Shabbat service and to study on Sunday afternoons. His first struggles with Judaism became an issue only when it was being taken away from him. "I remember our first Christmas tree around the age of nine; my mother said it was a Chanukah tree. My mother was converting to Mormonism right under my father's nose." His mother was also having an affair with a Mormon man who lived down the block.

It was also around this time that his older sisters and brother began using drugs. "Our home was a flophouse for hippies," Yohannan said. "They'd come over, get loaded, and crash. We lived in constant fear, either from the weirdos in our home, the physical abuse from a now-very-alcoholic father, or from a mother who seemed more and more a stranger to us." It was also during this time that his older brother David, while under the influence of "reds," was hit by a semi-truck on the first day of summer of his twelfth year. "He stayed in a coma for five years," Yohannan said, "and though he came out of it, he is to this day in a convalescent home unable to talk, and does not know who we are anymore."

It was right after his brother's accident that his mother abandoned the family for her new man down the street. "She left a note on the kitchen table for the older children to find and read to the younger ones," Yohannan said. "I was around ten years old." His father hired women to take care of the younger children as the older girls left home. That's when the sexual abuse started. "It did not happen much to me, but it did with the younger ones. I only remember his woman touching me inappropriately—I told my father, and she was fired, but only after she lived with us for four or five months."

Because his father could not take care of the three remaining children, they went to live with relatives. "I was sent to my grandparents from my mother's side of the family, which was not a bad thing, only they had converted to Mormonism, too, and from the moment I walked through their door, it was made very plain to me that there would be no more Jewish business going on."

Yohannan was expected to attend church and go to seminary. It was church and Sunday school that he hated most because there was nothing he understood or could relate to. Life with his grandparents was not horrible, just very different and lonely. "There was little conversation; they had already raised their children, and I knew I was interrupting someone's plans.

"In my thirteenth year, my father contacted me and asked if I wanted to come live with him again." His father said he had remarried, that Yohannan had a stepbrother and stepsisters, that the family was back together now except for him, and that he would buy Yohannan a drum set—something he had always wanted and never had. "My father picked me up about a week before Christmas. On the way to the house, he told me all about his restaurants, Kentucky Roast Beef and Hamburger Ding-A-Ling, but little did I know that at the age of thirteen, I'd be working almost full time to help support the family." Directly after school, all the children would work with him until eleven at night, as well as working full days on the weekends.

Life with his father and new family (three girls and an older boy) was terrible. His siblings hated each other, did not want him in their home, and did not want his father married to their mother—for good reason. "My father was still an alcoholic, and his new wife was also an alcoholic. The children were on drugs. I remember being injected with LSD on two occasions by my stepbrother while I slept." He woke to the sting of a needle in his backside and then was on a trip for seven to ten hours, an experience he couldn't stand. The same stepbrother loved taking shots at the younger ones with his CO_2 BB gun. "I still have scars on my stomach," Yohannan says.

It was about then that he "began expressing anger in ways that were not normal." He would get into fights almost every day at school, and when he walked home from work, he would look for ways to get into fights, or some other trouble like stealing or vandalism, for what seemed to be no reason but that he was filled with rage.

"I lived a double life," he says. "I was quiet and demure at home, and a stuttering terror in public." During Easter vacation at the age of fourteen, he and his brother broke every window at his junior high school. For weeks, they were interrogated by the police, and eventually, his brother confessed. "I washed windows every day after school for two years to pay that bill," he says.

Yohannan and his family moved just about every year from age nine on, and he went to a different school every year in junior high and high school. He ran away from home a lot in his elementary school years but never got very far. Then at age fifteen, he tried to really run away, sleeping in parks for weeks until he was caught by the police. He contacted his grandparents and went to live with them until he was eighteen, when he moved out and got an apartment.

It was during this time that he committed his first crime, which resulted in being sent to the California Youth Authority facility at the Youth Training School (YTS) in Chino for three and a half years for "armed robbery with a gun and brandishing the gun." "YTS was called gladiator school, and for good reason—there was not a day that I did not have to fight," Yohannan says. When he was released, though he vowed never to commit another crime and return to prison, "I was a ticking time-bomb full of rage, and I had no coping skills to deal with my anger." He was working in construction, a job that began while he was on a YTS furlough, but he lost it within a few weeks because he wouldn't do his boss's personal gardening at his home.

Then, he got a job with a law firm as a paralegal, and started dating Mona, who had an eighteen-month-old son named Charles. "This was not a good situation; I was a stuttering time-bomb—I did not have the maturity or patience to be in a relationship, and especially with a young child." Everything set him off, and within weeks of beginning their relationship, Yohannan was violent toward Mona and Charles. "I began exhibiting frustration and anger in ways that were unwarranted and inappropriate to any situation that did not conform to my liking," he says.

He was especially violent toward Charles. "I could not comprehend nor could I understand then what I believed to be Mona's lack of discipline concerning Charles, and from my own distorted perspective, I saw Charles as a disobedient and defiant child who needed a strong hand and a good spanking." There were incidents in which he punched his fist through a wall or would stomp out of the house for anything that didn't agree with him, and he would go into a yelling rage that turned violent. "My anger was escalating, although I thought I could control it," he said.

After every incident, he swore he would never do it again, and believed that he could control himself. He and Mona discussed ways to handle the situation. "The harder I tried to control my anger, the worse I became. Everything would now set me off, and I would erupt in anger in ways that I hated—spanking, slapping, and hitting Charles."

About one o'clock one summer morning, after helping Mona move into a new apartment, he offered to take Charles home for the night to give her a break. All went well until around seven the next morning when he was getting Charles ready to return home to Mona. "Much to my frustration, Charles was fussy and would not stop crying," Yohannan said. "This angered me, and spanking Charles did not help matters. It only enraged me more, and in a flash, I hit Charles with a closed fist in the stomach."

What happened next was "an out-of-body experience that I watched and could not stop." He called Mona and told her what he had done, and that he needed help, that he couldn't handle the situation. "When I hung up the phone and starting getting ready to go, Charles did not respond to me. I held him to my chest, I cried, I screamed, I tried mouth-to-mouth, but nothing helped. I called the fire department; I knew I had hurt him badly. So I went to the hospital holding onto the back of the fire engine." Charles was dead.

Yohannan remembers telling a police officer that he had hit Charles "because he rejected me—I wanted us to be a family, I so wanted to have this relationship work, but Charles kept rejecting me, and that angered me.

"I destroyed his life, and everyone connected to Charles, to Mona, and to me. The world changed, Mona's world, my family's world, my world—it became a nightmare that would not end. I was sentenced to fifteen years to life for second-degree murder."

It is impossible to describe all the many experiences and different levels of growth and change that Yohannan went through during thirty-two years in prison. "I can only say that since I committed my crime, I have been horrified, ashamed, and profoundly remorseful for taking the life of Charles," he said, "and for the irredeemable damage and pain I caused to the many victims of my actions. In taking a life, I destroyed a world; I affected and altered people's lives beyond measure."

Since the moment he walked into prison, he has strived to come to terms with his actions, and in that process, he says, "I availed myself of every program in prison that would help me to understand my core issues, how and why I could commit such a crime." He wanted to obtain the tools and insights necessary to never harm anyone again.

As he looked back, Yohannan continued his efforts to "redefine myself—to grow in my spirituality and in my commitment and involvement to my community and toward individual lives wherever I am." He has spent the "past thirty-two years doing *T'shuvah* [a Torah-based concept of repentance that involves a true change of the heart]—and acting upon that responsibility with an infinite desire to repair the harm I cause to humanity and, I believe, the universe."

Yohannan has been active in voluntary group therapy and self-help programs both inside and outside prison walls; violence prevention; restorative justice; hospice care; serving the physically handicapped; and now being a part of a recovery program in which he can continue helping others and himself to grow. "One important thing I learned in prison is that every single person has value, and that everyone has a spark of divine godliness within them, and that spark of holiness obligates me to treat everyone with love and dignity."

Yohannan believes that even an "ungrateful, hateful person, righteous or evil, grateful or thankless, an unwanted guest, a person that is totally dependent on someone else's generosity, is still a holy person in beggar's clothing. A human being is royalty, and I must appreciate and honor the majesty of every person I encounter, because I am all of these things."

For many years, he could see that spark of holiness in others but not in himself. He could not forgive himself for what he had done. He had been considered for parole thirteen times by the state Board of Prison Terms, yet did not advocate for his own release. Often, the board would tell him, "The only one keeping you in prison is yourself!" Eventually, it became evident that spending the rest of his life in prison was not necessary and did not serve any purpose—although it was exactly what he had resigned himself to doing: "I had given up any thoughts of ever getting out, and began living the best possible life I could inside prison and with the people that were a part of my life."

Yohannan's determination to be a better person was evident in his activities and interactions throughout his prison term. He also returned to his religious roots and became an observant Jew. After his father died in 1986, he felt ashamed that he no longer knew what it meant to be a Jew, and knew nothing about his heritage or the observance of his faith. So he began reaching out to the Jewish community in prison wherever he was.

"I attended every Shabbat, and every holiday," Yohannan said. "I read over three thousand Jewish books: Torah, Talmud, Midrash, Zohar, Kabbalah, and every commentary from Rambam to Fromm. I was also the first Jew in San Quentin to don a *yarmulke* and *tzitzit* and walk the mainline." Fellow inmates would call him "the Jewish Beacon of San Quentin." It was not because he was a pillar but simply because Jews would see him, and it became safe to be Jewish in San Quentin.

"The Jews were respected," he said. "I do not take all the credit for that. Every Jew that 'came out' made it OK for the next Jew to be open and observant in whatever way they wanted to be." For too long, it was not safe to be Jewish in prison, especially at San Quentin, but in time, a "critical mass" was reached that gave the Jews enough visibility and presence. Where there once were only four, there were about fifteen Jews when he left there.

Yohannan was found suitable for parole and released in 2010. He was told on a Friday that he would be leaving prison the following Monday. "I am learning to live all over again," he says, "and life continues to be difficult and challenging. I do not take my freedom for granted, not for a moment." He sees that there is "unbelievable beauty in the world, even when life is not pretty—I am able to learn and be grateful, and in everything I do, there is a choice, there is freedom of will, and if I ask, I will be assisted by G-d in doing good."

Now, Yohannan lives in a Jewish halfway house community, which he finds can be both good and bad. "I love it here," he says, "and I also can't wait to get my feet on the ground and have my own home." When he first got out, he would get up early in the morning to pray, but for some reason, "I kept falling over—I would lose my balance and fall over. I'd get up and continue my prayers rocking back and forth and falling over. It took me a few more times to figure it out. You see, I was not used to standing on carpet. I had only stood and walked on concrete for over thirty-two years, and the soft carpet was making it difficult to walk or stand on, and especially to pray on." But he's getting used to it now. "I treat my freedom as a gift," he says, "and I am ever mindful of my blessing every moment, and I continue to do *T'shuvah*."

Bruce is a black man who had been raised a Christian. While in prison, he discovered that he had a Jewish grandmother, and decided to explore that part of his ethnic heritage. He, too, wore a *yarmulke*, and seemed an anomaly as a black man wearing such a specifically Jewish symbol. He and Yohannan were "cellies," or cell mates, and had taken to praying and studying together to learn Hebrew and how to read the Torah.

Their bar mitzvah was held in the small chapel, with about twenty guests they had invited. The bar mitzvah "boys" took us through the prayers, read from the *parashah,* their portion of the Torah, and explained it. It was a profound experience for me, having seen so many bar mitzvahs for nonincarcerated people. Never had any been so significant to me. I began weeping when I entered the chapel and continued to do so until we all threw the sweet candies at them, which is the ritual of celebration that comes at the end of the service. I was touched as I watched two men embrace their religion and honor the traditions that I had been brought up with. And here we were in such an unlikely setting.

The other noteworthy Jewish events in prison were the Passover Seders. These are led by the chaplain, who brings in foods and sets a lovely table for the service. The ritual follows the traditional order but is enhanced with singing by some of the more-talented prisoners, who lead the group in songs as well as dramatizations and interpretations. It is ironic that although part of the Seder speaks of the Jews in Egypt being imprisoned—exactly the setting in which the ritual dinner is being held—no one mentions the similarities between the historical Jews and these contemporary incarcerated prisoners.

The foods of the prison's Seder are the traditional ones, but because only sealed packages can be brought in, there is only boxed matzo, canned gefilte fish, and nuts. Grape juice is served because wine is not allowed. It is a meager repast and bears little resemblance to the feasts that those of us on the outside are accustomed to at Seders. Nonetheless, these services were quite powerful since I was spending them in a unique setting with men to whom their religion meant far more than it does to most people I had spent Seders with in the free world.

Moishe, now in his 60s, had served many years for killing his wife in an altercation. For him, Judaism is a way of life, and so is "doing life." He notes that, "The former is steeped in tradition and family; the latter is defined by rules, regulations, and an unfeeling bureaucracy." Moishe asked himself how a Jewish inmate can maintain his faith in such a sterile environment. "The answer comes from within," he said. "While it takes a *minyan* to technically maintain a Jewish community, this is often not attainable within the highly segmented prison structure. So, for starters, one must learn to do with less." Then, there is the minimal availability of rabbinical supervision. While many of California's older, centrally located prisons have at least a part-time Jewish chaplain, other prisons have none. "For many Jewish prisoners," Moishe says, "this means that survival of one's faith becomes a personal, almost-private commitment. And tempering one's desire to reach out to find other Jews is the awareness that Jewish minorities are an easy target for self-serving, violent prison gangs."

Moishe says that "to their credit, CDCR maintains recognition of Judaism as a core faith. To the extent of budget and rabbinical availability, it provides chapel space, kosher meals, and a place in the prison community." But what is missing is "the rich culture of Jewish family—only the bare essentials for the practice of religion." Nonetheless, Judaism survives behind the walls. Weekly services occur (not always on Shabbat because of limited staff resources) so that participants can ground their practice in the Torah. "Often," Moishe says, "inmates take the weekly Torah portion and write a commentary, which is shared with fellow congregants. Private study sessions are available with the chaplain. Jewish books are available for reading in the chapel library."

Jewish holidays take front and center stage for most Jewish inmates. Moishe notes that, "While vivid memories of family Seders, Simchas Torah dances, and Hanukkah parties are not replaced by the unpretentious prison offerings, the thought is there to stimulate one's memories." He adds that, "Perhaps the most solemn of rites, Yom Kippur, is best appreciated by those who arguably have the most to repent for."

Moishe tells of his many years during the 1970s and early '80s in the California Medical Facility at Vacaville, where he was kept in an "administrative hold" because of his electrical engineering skills. A rabbi was the most beloved of the prison chaplains there, and after he left, there was a five-year absence of any Jewish chaplain. "In this period," Moishe said, "Jewish inmates, under the voluntary supervision of the Protestant chaplain, were permitted to conduct their own services, and the community survived." He tells movingly that "when my father died, the Catholic chaplain immediately took down from the altar the giant votive candle and placed it in the Jewish chaplain's office where it burned continuously for a week, so that I could sit shivah."

He also tells of outside volunteers who catered fully kosher Seders at Vacaville for seventeen years—an incredible *mitzvah* (good deed). He says that "at San Quentin, the Jewish chaplaincy was more complex. Within the prison's highly segmented populations—reception center, administrative segregation, death row, the mainline, the 'ranch,' and the short-timer dorm unit—any services provided had to be administered separately."

The most "open" services, accessible to anyone of any religion, were with the "mainline" population in North Block, where over five hundred lifers lived. "From this population, four to ten men would come to weekly services," Moishe said.

"Most were approved by the chaplain for the kosher meal program. Holiday services and limited traditional food items were provided in the chapel at this time. Hanukkah candles (a contraband item in prison) were provided to be lit in the lieutenant's office in North Block each night." Even prisoners segregated in isolation cells were administered to weekly in individual visits to their cells by the chaplain.

"Notwithstanding any of these efforts to provide Jewish life to prisoners, the prison system frustrated many of the chaplain's efforts," Moishe said. Often, the mechanical, unfeeling actions of lockdowns led to scheduled events such as Jewish holiday celebrations being canceled, and not rescheduled. Likewise, sudden closures due to low fog that kept guards from seeing other towers, disease outbreaks, racial strife—even staff "sick-ins"—gave Jewish inmates a constant reminder of the realities of "doing life."

But "in spite of all the drama attending prison life, and its drag on the practice of Jewish life," Moishe said, "there were bright moments to be heralded," like the San Quentin bar mitzvah celebrations which were described and published proudly in the prison newspaper. "The Jewish chaplain reached out far beyond just congregants behind the walls," he said, "and, in the true spirit of mitzvah, offered succor and comfort to all who wished a voice of compassion. It is perhaps in this light that today, at San Quentin, Judaism is best respected among all prisoners for what it has been throughout the ages—an endearing and enduring way of life."

Clearly reading and listening to the words of lifers like these is a window into a world most of us never see or understand. It helps us see that there is light in this darkness, and that people can grow and change in such an environment even in the face of adversity. The experience has a great impact on those of us who work with the self-help groups at San Quentin but also has an incredibly important effect on the men who participate. They are changed—undeniably—by their contact with the outside world, with those of us who see their humanity and treat them as people to be respected, no matter what their crimes were.

Their voices have more to say as they describe their backgrounds, life experiences, crimes, prison life, and rehabilitation.

Chapter 4

The Prisoners' Voices

Going into prison means that you leave your normal life behind and open yourself to a completely existential world, meeting people who are remarkable in their diversity and complexity. Sometimes, it feels otherworldly. What I have found inside the walls of prison is that these men have gone through profoundly different life experiences than those with which most of us are familiar. When they tell me their stories, I realize how privileged and lucky I have been. My life has been easy compared with the lives most of these men have lived. I feel moved by the difficulties under which they grew up.

The other remarkable thing is watching the transformation of people who have committed horrible crimes and come to realize the profound effect their actions have had on others. John Irwin's fascinating study of *Lifers: Seeking Redemption in Prison* (Routledge, 2009) focused on fourteen guilty men incarcerated for life, with the possibility of parole, and discovered the phases that the redemption process takes. He describes "awakening" as the first stage—when the lifers fully appreciate what their past behavior was like and that it has brought them to "disastrous ends" (p. 66). Here, they take an inventory of their actions and see that even if they are released, they will continue down the same path unless something is done. This process can start early in their incarceration or much later. But without it, rehabilitation does not succeed and change does not occur. Since many of the inmates' crimes were committed as young men, when their consciences were ill-formed, Irwin says, it can take years before they are ready for this self-awareness.

He also says that transformation will not occur if a prisoner is immersed in the criminal belief system that allows for killing certain classes of people, or is enmeshed in the "yard shit," also called "the mix," of gambling, fighting, and assassination (p. 67). Often, religion, self-help programs, or the prison education system can lead to awakening.

Once this occurs, a prisoner begins to seek educational or vocational training, and other helpful programs. But since this type of programming often has been cut because of budgetary constraints and a "get tough on crime" attitude in the criminal justice system, it is hard to come by. In California, there is only a GED program in most prisons, with San Quentin being unique because of the Prison University Project. Vocational training programs are spotty, offered only when an instructor is available (p. 79). Often, it is hard to obtain supplies and equipment. Nonetheless, in some prisons like San Quentin, many volunteers help men who want to work on themselves find a way to self-awareness and redemption.

After awakening comes atonement. The prisoners begin to express extreme remorse and work on atoning for the pain they have caused others (p. 88). In this stage, they take full responsibility for what they have done, and within the programs they are participating in, begin to see their faults and shortcomings. Irwin describes this process as looking at their self-centeredness, selfishness, irresponsibility, and immaturity. After this, they begin to accept responsibility and have some kind of "socially beneficial orientation" (p. 88).

Irwin suggests that within the atonement phase, three distinct processes occur. First is the self-assessment or inventory, which involves looking more deeply into oneself and beginning to overcome some of the self-deception that has taken place over the years. The next process is evolving into a "good person" (p. 94). By looking at motivation and behavior, prisoners can eventually grow into caring, thoughtful, and responsible people who understand "their personal traits, weakness, propensities that led to them committing a serious crime, and a view of society that recognizes that all people are humans worthy of respect and are interconnected and dependent on each other" (p. 94).

Finally, after these changes occur, the prisoner begins to plan for life after release and engages in some kind of service work while still inside (p. 98). More often than not, the lifers decide to work with youths, since they themselves first got into trouble as young men. They feel compelled to give back to the society that they wronged. Sometimes, the public outside does not trust this attitude, thinking it is a facade taken on to help a prisoner obtain parole. However, of the inmates I've met who are now out, some studying for B.A. degrees and all working with service agencies in some way, none has returned to prison or gotten into any trouble since his release.

The story of Don Baylor, the New Leaf on Life leader introduced in chapter 3, illustrates this path. Born in 1951 in Minden, Louisiana, he moved to California with his parents at the age of four. The next year, though, his mother moved to Richmond, California, and became a Jehovah's Witness, while his father stayed in Los Angeles and "started pimping."

Don grew up moving back and forth between his parents while his two brothers stayed with his mother. "By the time I was eight, I had a shoeshine stand in front of my father's process shop [a hair salon specializing in perms for black men].The clientele were all pimps, dope dealers, bookies, and black mafia dudes. My father's closest buddies were named Gas, Gangster, Frank, Whispering George, Slim, and Big Bernie."

Although he never joined a gang, Don was always fascinated with the so-called "players' life." But the time he spent with his mother kept him from going all-out in their direction, since he did believe in God and knew there would be consequences, sooner or later, for "living the life."

Because both parents moved a lot, he went to several elementary schools and was never able to finish high school. He quit in the middle of the twelfth grade. "When I lived with my mother," Don says, "I tried to be a good Jehovah's Witness, but when I was with my father, he only respected hustlers and players, so I tried to be that.

"The first time I got high was when at the age of nine, I used to sweep the floors and empty the ashtrays at my father's hair shop, so since I had seen my pop's friends snorting the powder off of the album covers and putting fire to the joints, I saved up a bunch of powder and all of the roaches in the ashtrays until I had a nice amount for me and my friends to do together at the park."

One Saturday afternoon, Don and "Hooks, Boxhead, Smiley, and Gordon went to Gramercy Park in L.A. and snorted the powder and smoked the roaches. I liked it, so that was the beginning of the end."

That end came when, "one day, while staying in L.A. visiting relatives and working my hooker, I went to a liquor store on

Washington and Third Avenue when a guy ran up to me, telling me to get off of his corner." Don ignored him and went into the store, but the man blindsided him on the way out. "As an automatic response, I stabbed him in his neck. I had no idea that I had hit his carotid artery, nor was it my intention to kill him. I stabbed him one time.

"I committed my crime in December 1989. I spent two years in L.A. County Jail fighting the murder charge. A jury found me guilty of second-degree murder, and I was sentenced to fifteen years to life. I have been to the parole board four times: 1998, 2005, 2008, and 2010, each time deemed unsuitable for parole. My next scheduled hearing is April, 2013."

To Don, "being in prison has been a terrible experience. I do not know how anyone could do anything to fully come back from this experience, because I know that I never will. I hate virtually every waking moment, other than when I am on a visit, at our New Leaf on Life group, or running a food sale. Those are literally my only good experiences."

Don likes John Irwin's ideas but says that "for me, atonement came first." After coming to prison, he realized that if he had "always listened to my mother, I would not be here. I am always troubled by the fact that I am responsible for the loss of human life." In his two years in the county jail, he read the Bible from cover to cover four times. "So when I got to prison, I decided to quit using drugs. I actually stopped using cocaine and heroin in the county jail." He decided on New Year's Eve of 1991 that he would drink his last cup of "pruno" (a prison wine fermented from apples, oranges, fruit cocktail, ketchup, sugar, and any other useful ingredient) and smoke his last joint. "I did accomplish that," he says. "I believe that all of the prayers helped me stop.

"As for programs that helped me to wake up and decide that I wanted to live the square life if I ever get out, I would say they were the VORG, Narcotics Anonymous, and New Leaf on Life."

Don's life has taken a good turn in prison. He has learned skills in the law and writing court-related documents. And maintaining regular communication with the mother he loves deeply has helped give him the will to make it inside because he wants to see her on the outside before she dies. He sees his children and grandchildren through regular visitation and is attending college as well as self-help groups. He is the primary leader of New Leaf on Life, organizing the food sales that raise funds for outside service organizations as well as keeping the group's paperwork straight. Don works hard every day on understanding what drives him and how to become "a better person."

Little Man is a lifer who wrote an essay seeking forgiveness for his past from the community at large. In it, he said: "My world growing up in the South was infested with some love but mostly hatred, racism, alcoholism, guns, pain, abuse, death, and uncertainty. Nigger! Nigger! Nigger! My identity as a nigger, beatings after beatings, my identity was beatings. Fight! Fight! Fight!" And his identity was to fight as well. "But I was only a child trying to be a child who had no choice about what people said I was." He knew that his mother loved him unconditionally, telling him he was "her loving child, her son, her baby. I was one of her blessings from God."

Little Man also knew that his dad loved him; he told him so. "He would play football with me and the neighborhood kids. He would give me a good night kiss on my forehead. He taught me how to shoot a gun. He protected our family at night when white people would egg our home and throw rocks." To Little Man, "I had the best dad in all the world. He taught me to drive a car and encouraged me not to be afraid to talk to girls. Monday to Friday, my dad was my father and was my mother's great love."

But on weekends, when his father would drink, Little Man

asked himself "who was this person I loved and now had to fight to protect my whole family from? Who was this stranger with a knife in his hand trying to cut my mother's throat? Who was this man who my sister, brother, and I had to jump on to keep from killing our mother?" When alcohol fueled his father's rage, his mother became his personal punching bag.

"As a little boy, I had to become Little Man; the little boy had to die or else see his family ruined by alcohol, racism, and hatred. The years of my father's yelling, the blood all over my mother, the tears I cried as I saw him abuse her, the beatings did not allow me to stay a little child. So I learned to pray and ask God to bless me to get old enough to protect my mother from my daddy."

He became responsible for the health and safety of everyone he loved. "I was the protector, the man of the house. I was responsible for my baby brother, protecting him even if he had done wrong. I was responsible for keeping my mother safe even if it meant hurting my dad." This is the person he had to become.

The toll of his childhood experiences left Little Man deeply damaged: hated for being black, hit with rocks and bottles, years of his mother's abuse by her husband. "Seeing my mother's blood as she held the blade of my dad's knife in her hand, trying to stop him from cutting her throat, numbed me, and I began to believe that people were all predators of the weak." He was eighteen when he saw his mother almost killed, and it was "the first day my parents heard me curse. I told my dad that I was tired of this 'shit,' and I encouraged him to come and fight me. I had become a threat to his manhood."

To his father, "I was the 'nigger' he was called by whites." Little Man felt rejected, uneducated, and ignorant. "This was the day I gave my father six to eight stitches in his head. Later, I would fire a gun behind my father's feet when he tried to get a gun from the trunk of his car. I had now become his inner rage!

"I know now that all we had was each other, and that my father loved me. He was insulted and mistreated as a black man, and he carried the pain and hurt but could not show it, or he would not be a man. No, he had to wear the mask of toughness; a man is not supposed to cry."

Little Man learned that "in order for me to experience God's love, I must begin the healing process of first loving myself in order to be able to forgive others. I have forgiven myself for thinking that I had no place in life; I know that I do." He believes that if he had not gone through what he did, he would not have moved to California and met the love of his life. "I am truly happy. While incarcerated, I have adopted a child from the Congo. I am extremely grateful to God that you are my dad," he wrote in his essay, "and I have forgiven you with all my heart. God is in control, and I have accepted my trials and tribulations. God has promised to never leave me or forsake me."

Little Man has taken full responsibility for his crimes and the harm he caused his victims. "I took the life of their loved one and caused unwanted suffering to their families. I have a responsibility to my family, my friends, to people who hate me, and to my community to demonstrate that I am not just a product of my environment, or the label placed on me by others."

He writes in his essay of his desire to become a beacon of hope for others in this world. "Little Man made some awful choices," he says in conclusion, "which have caused so much grief and pain to others. I forgive that small child and thank God for being born black and loving. I am somebody and am loved and appreciated. Dear God, help me to help you to help me forgive."

Little Man's story shows the stages described by Irwin: the understanding of the person he was, the understanding of the pain he has caused, the self-awareness of how he became a criminal, and the process of redemption and atonement. It has been years in process, but a successful process nonetheless.

Jinryu, the Buddhist prisoner who discovered meditation in prison and told part of his story in chapter 3, also described his youth and some of his prison life in a personal essay. His process of atonement and redemption continues on a daily basis, as he so movingly illustrates. "Early in my childhood," Jinryu says, "I recall being asked to choose who I would like to live with, my father or mother. Living in my mother's parents' home, I ran to my grandfather, scared and uncertain of what was going on."

His father had many control issues, and brought home from the Korean War symptoms that we now probably would identify as PTSD, trying his best to deal with his pain without the proper tools. "This vivid incident [in which he had to choose a home] changed the safeness of my world. Each summer, I was sent off to relatives or later summer camps. These served to further allow me to stuff my feelings of alienation, fear and loneliness."

Most of his childhood remains a fog, Jinryu says. What he remembers most "was isolating my feelings and problems from everyone around." With the legal drinking age at eighteen in New York in the early '70s, he used false identification and learned how to overcome his awkwardness and feelings with alcohol. It stayed a major part of his life until he finally could quit in 1981. "In my search for self," he says, "I looked outside of myself."

On December 20, 1978, I committed the crime I told you about earlier. The ripples of each bullet as it penetrated my victim ended his dreams for a peaceful and productive life. I caused suffering not only to my victim but to his family, friends, and countless others. This suffering continues to cascade into the future.

Instead of taking responsibility and turning myself in to the Marine Corps, where I was a sergeant and military instructor, I fled. In 1983, I was arrested and charged with kidnap to commit robbery, robbing, attempted murder, to name a few charges. Sentenced to life with possibility of parole, once known as seven years to life, I have served over twenty-six years. I became eligible for parole in 1991 and have been denied since then. I received a three-year denial in 2009 and have now been eligible for over nineteen years, with still little hope of getting out.

Jinryu's first prison was Folsom State, "a place where fear, anger, hurt, and loneliness were the norm. I have never witnessed so much violence and inhumanity. What is the value of human life in prison?" He saw people stabbed in the yard. He watched as shots were fired and whistles sounded. "Everyone dropped to the ground. A gurney took the man who was stabbed away; another man was handcuffed and removed from the yard. An officer on a catwalk yelled below, 'Play ball.' Life went on."

Jinryu describes how "a few days later, a man in the cell next to me was stabbed over one hundred times before anyone responded. The walls of the cell were coated with his blood. He died two months later. To escape the hell realm, I would daydream to avoid reality. Folsom State Prison was a killing zone in the 1980s."

In subsequent prisons, Jinryu began attending programs such as A.A., anger management, therapy groups, stress and relaxation, meditation, victim offender education, alternatives to violence, and New Leaf on Life. He worked hard and "was fortunate in 2008 to receive a four-year [B.S.S.] degree from Ohio State University."

Jinryu says that his "atonement" is very much linked to his spiritual practice. "I once read that the purpose in life is to work on oneself and to be of service to others. In Buddhist practice, there is a verse chanted each full moon service: 'All my ancient twisted karma, from beginningless greed, hate, and delusion, born of body, speech, and mind, I am now fully aware.' "

Simply put, he feels responsible for all the suffering and pain he has caused and continues to cause others. Jinryu holds himself accountable. As he moves along the path of self-improvement, teachers appear everywhere. "I have been fortunate to be incarcerated at San Quentin," he says, "where programs are abundant and community members bring their knowledge and support to help us improve ourselves and assist us in becoming pro-social. My atonement is in the service of others, as I make my amends to those I have caused so much hurt and pain."

Jinryu is a delightful man to know. He is funny, smart, and a leader among his peers. With the ongoing support of his children, he has been successful inside the prison walls in making a life for himself and being a role model for many who encounter him.

Another prisoner, Black, has written "Mystory: A public educational experience" in which he tracks the failure of the public school system as it helped turn him into the criminal he became. He is a three-striker who is appealing his incarceration through the courts. Interestingly, he graduated valedictorian of his class while in prison.

Black told me that when he was labeled a dysfunctional student and placed in special ed classes in Winton, California, in the 1970s, being excluded from regular classes and contact with their students had a "crippling effect on my educational development. The stigma of being categorized a special ed student has left a scar deep in the gray matter of my heart. Not only has this misdiagnosis impacted me and my family, it has also warped the thinking and interaction of society toward me." He believes that his placement in special ed excluded him from learning normal social behaviors, interacting with his peers, participating in advanced education courses, graduating, and learning skills needed for employment and job advancement.

"I believe my exclusion from appropriate public education," Black says, "both contributed to and influenced the criminal activity in my life that eventually carried me away from the American dream and on a path to incarceration."

> I was labeled a special ed student, dysfunctional and stereotyped as deviant, hostile and oppositional. My lack of enthusiasm for education and no doubt my [African-American] skin color, along with the simple child-like trouble I would get into, seemed like the logical justifications for my placement in such classes. As a child, I knew something was different about me, and this became evident in how I was treated in school. Trying to find my self-identity, I rebelled in the only ways I knew how, such as being disruptive and picking on other children to get attention. In my mind, there was no reason to apply myself due to a lack of motivation. Consequently, I fell into a trap and reinforced the negative labels that were put upon me. I rebelled and acted in ways that exemplified a dysfunctional, stereotypically deviant, hostile child.

As a child, Black could never keep his hands off other people's things. He took from his mother's purse and would "borrow" money from his sisters, hoping they would never know. "In high school," he says, "I would take things from the 7-Eleven, like two-liter sodas and Doritos, to impress my football buddies." Eventually, he graduated to burglary, taking money from a grade-school fund-raising sale. From there, he advanced to burglarizing houses and then kicking in doors for strong-arm robbery of drug dealers. The two counts of robbery and burglary for breaking into the drug-house were what led to his third strike.

Assigned to a "sports curriculum" in high school because of his above-average athletic skills, Black was encouraged to play sports at the expense of his education. But after a hernia as a sophomore kept him from playing football, "my failure to succeed in sports, my poor attendance, and my failing grades resulted in my expulsion from high school. The next year, I was bused to a continuation school designated for low-achieving students." It offered no challenge, and was somewhere it was easy to get marijuana, speed, and cocaine. Black also drank beer regularly and stole to support his alcohol and drug abuse, finally dropping out of school.

> In that continuation school, I was among the most negative students in the school district. The rate of expulsion and dropping-out was phenomenal. This school became a crucible for the development of my criminal mindset. As a dropout, I gravitated toward other dropouts. Without a structured educational environment, the long-term effects of being an uneducated dropout were underemployment, drug use, involvement in criminal behavior, and an increasing chance of incarceration.
>
> As a young black man, I was monitored by police as a fact of life. My label as a dysfunctional student rolled into being labeled as a criminal. I

was about fourteen years old when I had my first run-in with the police. One evening returning from watching the Friday night varsity football game, I was about a block away from my house when I was stopped by the sheriff. I was asked what I was doing out after curfew. Fearfully, I explained where I was coming from and where I was going. I was taken in to the sheriff's department, and my mother was called to come and pick me up. They had impressed upon her that I needed supervision—implying I was deviant, hostile, and oppositional. They suggested that she contact the probation office to find help for her son. She discovered, as a single mother, that this would not be the last time her son would be placed in the back of a police car.

Incarcerated for many years of his life, Black had the fortitude to pick up some good behaviors from the programs offered in prison. He enrolled in GED classes while incarcerated, and when he was paroled in 1993, his mother motivated him to take the GED test. To his surprise, he passed.

In 1990, he had enrolled in a pre-release class with instruction on life skills, setting goals, and achieving success. As a result, he had a short period of success. He bought a car before being released on parole and collected resources to obtain a job, a place to live, and a bank account within six months after getting out. "I successfully achieved all my goals," he says. "Yet without insight into my behaviors and reasons for criminal activity, I relapsed and found myself back in prison on a parole violation." But over time after that, a gradual awakening came to Black, and an awareness of what he had done.

> Having a change of mindset and a revelational insight into my criminal behavior, I fully understand the need to fully prepare incarcerated people for successful community reentry. For example, today I am a granddaddy. In addition, I care very much for my mama, my sisters, children, and everyone in my family. The person I was before redemption from a criminal mindset, I would not want that man living next to my loved ones. But as a redeemed prisoner, I know the value of life and have learned to appreciate and give of myself.

Black also found that "being under the structured academic tutelage of the Prison University Project and self-help programs at San Quentin, I have attained a solid educational foundation with resources and support." He has earned an associate of arts degree from Patten University and is working toward a bachelor's degree, hoping to go on and earn a master's in social work. Eventually, he would like to work in reentry programs to help others like himself achieve positive change in their lives—and people like his own son who has been thrown out of school. His son is in an independent studies program now, and Black is afraid that "he is being pushed further away from the importance of education and further onto the streets. I see myself in him."

He feels that "establishing a reliable and stable understanding of myself from the many self-help programs during my ten-year incarceration will no doubt benefit me as well as the many young men like my son." His success in finally completing programs for the first time in his life, as well as being class valedictorian, has spurred his desire to make further positive changes. "These programs at San Quentin have stimulated me," Black says, "and involved me in cultural norms and positive connections between myself, my family, and my community."

His story is a poignant one. One can only wonder what was driving him to be so difficult as a youth, and how, despite his intelligence, he was able to slip through the cracks of the school system. We might also ask about his need to steal, and why it became a compulsion even in the face of further incarceration. Black's tale is actually helpful as we begin to think about how to reach such young men before they enter prison.

Savio is a Mexican who had a happy childhood in a family with two brothers. He had what he needed to survive, and played soccer well. But he did not do well in school and "fell in with the wrong crowd." When he was seventeen, his family moved to San Diego. "I had gotten myself into a big mess in Mexico," Savio says, "which is why we had to move to California. It did not take too long to meet new people in the drug world. That took me into the life of crime."

By the 1970s, he started doing time in county jails, and in 1989, he went to prison for the first time. He was paroled, but in 1995, he came back to prison with a life sentence under the three-strikes law. His crimes were burglary and intent to commit burglary, but although he never injured anyone, he does not even have a parole hearing until 2019.

"All my cases are nonviolent thefts," he says, "and still I received a twenty-five-to-life sentence. I have now been in prison for seventeen years, and it will take at least eight more years until I am even eligible to go to the board. It looks like I am going to do at least twenty-five years and probably more for these nonviolent crimes. Now, people who commit these kinds of crimes get three years or less in prison."

Savio has been enrolled in many self-help programs, including New Leaf, an investment group, and anger management classes. He truly does not enjoy his factory work making mattresses, although the mindless escape appeals to some other inmates. "I am a good citizen in prison," Savio says, "attending all programs inside and trying to get along with everyone. I am an example of the consequences of the three-strike law, and hope the law will be overturned."

Mike, another regular member of New Leaf, is a member of many self-help groups, well-respected, and loved by his peers. His mother was divorced with four children when she married his father in 1952, the year Mike was born. She died of internal bleeding giving birth to his younger brother.

"As I have recently discovered," Mike says, "her death played an important role in my decisions in adolescence and adulthood." He has no memories of his mother except an old photograph he had for years of her in a black cowboy hat. "Nor do I have any memories of the four children she had before me. My father, on the other hand, was a different story. There are lots of memories of him—unfortunately, nearly all negative."

Mike's earliest memories were filled with anger, fear, frustration, and, most of all, loneliness. "For you see, my father was an alcoholic with a lot of demons, either real or imaginary, no patience, anger issues, and a violent temper. He was either in and out of prison, or we (myself, brother, and whatever woman he happened to be married to at the time along with her children) were on the move one step in front of the law."

By the time of Mike's thirteenth birthday, he had already had at least four stepmothers, lots of stepbrothers and stepsisters, and been in several foster homes as well as the juvenile hall and boys' homes. "I was a loner with no concept of belonging, love, or intimacy, and preferred it that way. That said, my notorious criminal history consists of running away the first chance I got and on one occasion, breaking into someone's home because I was cold and hungry."

As remarkable as he has been told it sounds, he has never been involved in any gang activity or used any kind of drugs or alcohol, and, "I have issues with those who do." Despite all that was going on, he still managed to graduate from high school and completed some college classes.

"At the age of seventeen," Mike says, "while on a camping trip, I met a young girl who was to become the love of my life, who I married and with whom I had two beautiful children." Unfortunately, "as wonderful as that sounds, in reality, it spelled doom. I was in no way ready for the responsibility—emotionally, mentally, or financially—to become a husband or father." He tried, but the future he had envisioned did not come to pass.

> In the early morning hours of December 11, 1978, my world as I had known it came to a crashing conclusion. In the parking lot of a closed service station lying on the ground dead was the same love of my life and mother of our two children. Not only did this senseless act of cruelty and violence cost her her life but it ruined and made many other lives nearly unbearable. There are different versions of what actually transpired that night, but the end result is still the same, and that is that I was and am responsible for the death of my own children's mother.

Nearly one year to the day later (December 10, 1979), Mike entered the state prison system. He was twenty-six years old and had been sentenced to twenty-five years to life plus an additional two years for the use of a firearm. He is still serving his time at the age of fifty-eight. Under the current system, to be released, he had to appear in front of a parole board panel and convince its members he is a changed man and that no circumstance could ever arise in which he would make poor choices or use poor judgment as he did in the past.

"Having made my initial board appearance and nine subsequent ones, I was not able to convince them," Mike says. "At the hearings in the past, the panel recommended that I stay discipline-free, participate in self-help groups with programs, and get chronos, all of which I have done."

The vagaries of parole boards are one of the givens that prisoners must accept and adjust to. Their recommendations can theoretically be overridden by the governor, but since he generally appoints members who have corrections backgrounds and share his own views, they tend to respond to the same political winds as the governor, which these days blow no logic or leniency toward the inmates.

Mike's hearings were initially two years apart, then went to one year, but after that, he received a three-year denial. Under current law, this is the automatic period any life prisoner found unsuitable for parole must wait for a new hearing unless the board reduces the minimum wait. "At the end of last year," Mike says, "I made my tenth subsequent board appearance. As in the past, I was optimistic that this would be the one." And it was! He is scheduled to be released in May 2012.

As he reflects back over the past thirty-two years of life on the inside, Mike says it has been an emotional roller coaster. "The ups and downs started at the very beginning when the old gray goose rolled up to the gates of Folsom Prison, after having spent fourteen hours on the road getting there. I sat in my cuffs and chains looking out the windows at those high, gray stone walls, thinking that my life was over. Even as my eyes began to mist over, I had already been schooled (in the county jail) that it was too late for tears and that tears were a sign of weakness."

He knew that if he was going to survive, it would take everything he had learned in county jail plus his own survival instincts. After a while, he began running on autopilot. "Whatever friends or family I had in the beginning stopped writing, accepting my collect calls, or visiting, and it caused my world to become condensed down to the immediate institution I happen to be in at any given time."

Mike's first real up in prison was getting remarried. "A friend of another inmate's wife started to write to me and then began visiting. After a year and a lot of discussion, we were married in the visiting room in front of friends and family. It was great." At the time, there were conjugal visits, which were a huge plus. But they have since been ended for lifers.

"I also got home-cooked food, an actual bath, not a shower, and, of course, the sex," Mike says. "This union allowed me to once again be connected to another human being. The marriage only lasted seven years, ending in divorce—an agreed-upon action because of the stresses put on any relationship; it was hard to be someone outside married to an incarcerated inmate."

For Mike, "the second real up was my discovery of Buddhism in 2002. The two simple concepts of interconnectedness and nonpermanence have been more of a blessing than I could ever give full credit to. The joy and the frustration of my practice always keeps me grounded, gives me a sense of self-worth and the knowledge that I belong."

There have been many downs while in prison, the biggest being the death of his cell partner's wife. They have been "cellies" for years, and her death, of natural causes, came without warning and was highly traumatic. "I was there for him and tried to give him as much privacy as possible so that he could grieve without having to face all the other prisoners." Many people dropped by to offer their condolences, but Mike stood guard and asked them to come back in a few days. "What stands out from that time was that not one of those hardened convicted felons objected to being sent away, and showed compassion and understanding."

The second-biggest down was the day in 2004 when he walked into the parole board hearing and saw on a monitor, after not hearing from any family member for twenty-five years, his son, daughter, and brother-in-law, sitting with an 8x10 picture of their mother prominently displayed on the table, for effect. It had quite an impact, and as he was asked many questions over the next four hours, he heard and began to see for the first time the harm, pain, and devastation he was responsible for causing. "The barriers I had put up crumbled, and the tears seemed like they would never stop. I was never the same person after that day."

Although Mike has been involved in self-help groups and had his practice, he knows now that that was not enough. "I began to actively pursue groups and programs that gave me the tools to not only recognize the poor choices I had made but an understanding of why I made them." First was the Victim Offender Reconciliation Group (VORG).

Within his first twenty minutes in the group, he knew he was in trouble. "You see, nobody told me how painful growing can be." VORG's first two rules were "everything that is said in this room stays in this room" and "no matter what feelings or emotions arise, you cannot leave." The curriculum was six months long, each group meeting with no more than ten inmates and an outside facilitator.

It was hard for Mike, sitting in a closed room with nine other inmates, sharing his past and showing emotion. "I looked around the room," he says, "and saw in their eyes and physical reactions that I was not alone in my trepidations. Nonetheless, I persevered, became a more-compassionate human being, and discovered the true meaning of empathy. Six years later, I am still an active member of the group and still growing. And yes, it is still painful."

He is in two other groups as well and hopes to remain so indefinitely. "One is New Leaf on Life where Dr. Leeder brings college professors and the like who are willing to share their expertise. It gives me an opportunity to interact with people I might never know. The topics are wide-ranging and always interesting, even if sometimes over my head. And that's OK because I have learned that being outside one's comfort zone can be a very rewarding experience."

The other group is Brothers' Keepers, which was founded in large part because of the suicide of an inmate whom a lot of prisoners knew but whose despair and pain they couldn't see. The sponsor is Bay Area Women Against Rape. These women come in for two hours every Monday in an attempt to help the prisoners help others. Primarily, the inmates learn about "active listening" and just being there for another person.

"A critical part of the curriculum," Mike says, "is learning to sit with someone who is in crisis, acknowledge that crisis, and try to assist them in formulating something that will allow them to cope with or bring some understanding to the situation. This is the group far outside the box for me and one which I struggle with weekly. I am determined to successfully complete it."

To Mike, "the person today is not anything like the person of old. My goals are to make a positive difference in the world. And that goal does not have to wait until I am released. In fact, it can't. I believe that if I can't make a positive difference in here, what chance do I have of making one on the outside?" His plans for life after release are simple, a lot like his practice. "I have made a commitment to myself to spend the remainder of my life in the service of others in whatever positive aspect that may be," Mike says. "I can never undo or make amends for the wrongs I did to my children and others. What can be done is for me to be the best possible person I can."

He hopes that by doing just that, rather than being a detriment to society, he can be a positive influence on anyone with whom he comes in contact. "I would eventually like to go into hospice care, either for those who need assistance or for those who are terminally ill. I can think of nothing more honorable than to be given the trust to be allowed to sit with and aid those who are unable to do for themselves, at a time when they might be most vulnerable and yet retain their dignity."

As you can see, these all are men who know the situations that led to their crimes, and have tried to overcome their pasts to become better human beings. My co-leader, John Kelly, has often called prison his "home away from home." His reflections on the years he's spent with people like these can help us understand what working in prison is like.

In February, 1991, he made his "very first visit inside San Quentin: trepidation, confusion, anticipation! What am I doing here? I spend four nights and three days with forty-two men in blue and thirty-five (visitors) from the outside." This was the Kairos Prison Ministry International, an intense spiritual weekend. On Monday night, he took part in "one of the most powerful, genuinely human experiences that I have ever had. The forty-two candidates share what the weekend meant to them before an audience of rooting, supporting, inside/outside enthusiasts. I cry! I freely and openly cry!"

John has taken part in thirty-one of the thirty-four Kairos weekends since then, and he is hooked. "I am hooked on San Quentin as a whole," he says. "It is truly my home away from home. I am in there two times a week, three times a week, sometimes more" with different groups. "I spend so much time in prison," John says, "that if I'm ever arrested, I will have already done my time."

Why? I see miracles. I see fellow human beings who have been transformed into some of the
finest people I know. What do I know now that
I did not know in 1991? There is not one ounce
of fear in me when I am inside those walls. I am
home. I realize that men in blue had been victims
in their own lives, especially in their early years. I
am often overwhelmed by the sheer horror that
some endured growing up, something that those
from stable households can't even imagine. To see
them as they are today is a powerful proof of the
ability of humans to change and grow. I often find
it hard to believe that they have committed some
horrendous acts. At the same time, their coming
to grips with the pain they have caused themselves and others becomes one of the driving
forces behind their will to change.

Yet John notes the reality that these observations "do not
apply to everyone in blue at San Quentin, not even the majority.
By the same token, San Quentin is the one prison in the State
of California that has an unbelievable array of programs, almost
entirely volunteer-driven, that allows anyone the opportunity to
change at any time. And sometimes it takes time."

An added miracle among those who have
changed is their intense commitment to help others on the inside to change, to help society at large
to understand them, and to help people on the
outside, especially youths, to avoid their fate. Some
of the most meaningful moments I have partici-
pated in inside are those that clearly focus on in-

mates challenging other inmates to think, to act, to speak in a new way. Chief among the movers and shakers are the lifers, the ones whose lives were the most pain-filled, whose transformations are the most profound. I tell my lifer friends that I want them to get out for two reasons: because they have earned it and because they have the wisdom that this world desperately needs. I could write a book about the wondrous things many parolees are doing in the world outside to keep young people from following a criminal path.

When John looks back on his fifteen years as a high school teacher, one of the most beautiful experiences was the unconditional love and acceptance he received from so many teenagers once they developed a sense of trust. "I have this experience all over again," he says, "every time I walk the grounds of San Quentin. I feel totally spoiled!"

Chapter 5

A Call for Change

Years ago when I was a young professor, I studied and then taught social policy at the undergraduate level. While teaching, I discovered that the best way to understand policy is through a theoretical analysis that would keep students from getting lost in all the trees without understanding the whole forest that the trees live in.

The most useful theory I used was the "incrementalism" approach of Charles Lindblom, a political science/public administration professor at Yale. Although he originally described the ideas in 1959, he updated them in 1979, and they are still relevant today, particularly relative to social policy concerning lifers. Public policies, Lindblom argues, are not well thought out and just "muddle through." Although we might like to think that social policies are rational, in fact, quite the contrary is true. Social policy is not about facts, efficiency, or being comprehensive. Instead, it is based on the fact that most of us (especially policy-makers) fear drastic changes and are more comfortable basing our decisions on our past practices.

Lindblom has said that policy is not made just once; it is made over and over again, especially as the policy-makers view the consequences of their choices, both positive and negative. Because they must adjust to so many pressures, and no one can have a complete analysis of any situation, policy is generally an attempt to simplify. Policy-makers tend to actually ignore the possibility of any big changes—ones that might be "outside the box" or not acceptable politically—because of the fear of being wrong, or of such changes' not being politically expedient. Because the policy-makers fear making big mistakes, they do nothing significant, they make no big changes or decisions, and we all live with the consequences of their caution. According to Lindblom, social policy generally is based on compromise, basically a conservative approach that is low risk and maintains the status quo.

This is what I would argue has happened with social policy relative to lifers. Because government policy-makers fear the repercussions of their decisions, particularly concerning people whom they view as having committed heinous crimes, they are afraid to risk letting such prisoners out. They are afraid of public backlash, and the consequence is that they are spending money needlessly on a population that is the least likely to reoffend.

In California, four sentences are possible for a murder conviction: the death penalty, life without parole, twenty-five years to life for first-degree murder, and fifteen years to life for second-degree murder. Actually, the often-used term "lifer" is a misnomer since the theoretical goal of incarceration is rehabilitation that prepares an inmate for release as soon as he is deemed ready and the parole board no longer considers him a danger to the community. Those with fifteen-to-life and twenty-five-to-life sentences are called Term to Life Prisoners and must be granted a parole hearing as soon as their minimum terms are completed.

This all sounds reasonable, except that the reality of the situation is quite the contrary. Of the 140,610 individuals serving life sentences in the United States—one out of every eleven inmates, or 9.5 percent of the prison population—41,095, or 29 percent, have no possibility of parole. That number has increased by 22 percent from 2003 to 2008 (Nellis and King, 2009), a growth rate four times that of the prisoners who are eligible for parole. Over 2.3 million people are currently in prison or county jails.

California alone has thirty-two thousand lifers in its prisons, only seventeen thousand of them there for murder convictions. The others are "three-strikers," some of whom are there for a third strike that was not a serious or violent crime. Many of these prisoners' felony offenses were minor ones, but as a result, the numbers of people incarcerated for three strikes rises every year. I knew one prisoner whose third strike was for stealing a pizza, yet he was now in prison without the possibility of parole!

One of the men we met earlier, Black, will never be eligible for parole even though none of his three felonies was violent. And lifers who were convicted of murder are being held for more than thirty years before parole even though they are eligible after twenty years for first-degree or twelve years for second. Clearly, Lindblom's analysis indicates that this is an incremental policy approach which leads to more years being added to lifers' time in prison because of political motivations, rather than being based on data or reason.

Lifers are less likely to reoffend than any other parolee. Of the 988 lifers released in California in the past twenty-one years, only six have reoffended (Dannenberg, 2011). What is also remarkable is that none of the six offenses were murder, which would have led to another life term. Stanford University found in a study in 2011 that on the average, convicted murderers in

California spend twenty years in prison and almost never commit new crimes after being released (Stanford University Criminal Justice Center, 2011). The study also found that because of tougher policies by parole boards, prisoners whose requests are denied now have to wait an average of five years for their next hearing, compared with two years for those denied in 2007.

One-fourth of the thirty-two thousand lifers in California were found to be eligible for parole, and lifers constitute one-fifth of the state's total number of prisoners. What is most interesting is that although the U.S. Supreme Court has ruled that prisoners should be evaluated by parole boards based on whether they are a danger to society rather than solely on the facts of their crime, the California board nevertheless often cites the "heinous" nature of the crime as its reason for denying parole.

In 2011, some California legislators tried to rescind the possibility of parole for lifers as a result of a case in which a paroled lifer kidnapped and held a child hostage for many years. These cases are quite rare, and yet the public and the legislature react as if such behavior is the norm. Data is what these decisions should be based on, not only public opinion and a knee-jerk reaction to win votes in an election year.

The use of life sentences has increased dramatically in the last twenty years, and life terms without parole have expanded as well. Since opponents of capital punishment have promoted life sentences as an alternative, more people are ending up in prison with no possibility of parole. These policies are motivated by a "get tough on crime" approach that has superseded the rehabilitation model of the past.

People who hear stories of paroled felons' reoffending become committed to retaliating against all criminals, even those who no longer are dangerous. Many advocates for long sentences are members of victim rights groups, prosecutors, and police associations, all claiming that public safety is at risk. In the federal system as well as Illinois, Iowa, Louisiana, Maine, Pennsylvania, and South Dakota, *all* life sentences have no possibility of parole *ever*! Over the last twenty-five years, the number of people serving life sentences has quadrupled, from 34,000 in 1984 to 140,810 in 2008 (Nellis and King, p. 6). In fact, because life terms without parole are recommended so often, the *New York Times* argued in an editorial September 13, 2011 that such sentences should be used only instead of giving people the death sentence. This is yet another example of how incrementalism has permeated policy-making.

Even when people become eligible for parole, governors and parole boards are reluctant to grant release. The national average of time served is twenty-three years, with some states requiring that people serve up to fifty years even when they are eligible for parole (Nellis and King, p. 6). In California, Governors Gray Davis and Arnold Schwartzenegger were notorious for overriding recommendations from their own parole boards that lifers be granted parole. In his five years as governor, Davis paroled only five lifers, and Schwartzenegger paroled 103 in eight years.

The last four governors before the current Jerry Brown—George Deukmejian, Pete Wilson, Davis, and Schwartzenegger—reversed recommendations for eight out of ten lifers found suitable by their own parole boards. According to the Stanford Criminal Justice Center's study, the likelihood that parole granted to a lifer with a murder conviction would *not* be overturned by the governor was just 6 percent in 2010. By contrast, Brown, who took office in 2011, has approved 80 percent of the board's decisions (Mullane, 2011). Of the seventeen thousand murderers among the lifers in California prisons, ten thousand are eligible for parole (Mullane, 2012). In addition, the state's parole boards have used their discretion to triple the amount of time between parole hearings from one to five years before 2009 to three to fifteen years now. Prisoners despair about ever being able to get out.

Incrementalism can also be seen in how the rules have changed while prisoners are incarcerated and serving the time they thought they were supposed to serve. Many lawsuits by prisoners have argued unsuccessfully that when judges sentenced them to life, parole was possible and they were usually eligible after twelve years, with parole actually taking place in sixteen years. Data from Michigan, for example, showed that from 1941 to 1974, 416 eligible lifers were paroled, about twelve a year. But in the last twenty-four years, the number of paroled lifers in the state declined to about seven a year (www.nytimes,com/2005m10.02.national/03life.web.html 7/19/11).

What has begun to happen is that people who once were given life sentences with the possibility of eventually going home now are dying in prison. The life sentence has become a death sentence instead. We are not seeking rehabilitation; we are now seeking incapacitation and isolation of people because their crimes repel us and they are thus deemed a threat. Is this what we want as a civilized society?

So what is the motivation for keeping such people in prison for longer than their minimum terms and making it less likely that lifers will be granted parole? Many argue that the reason is economic. The construction money and jobs drive governments to build prisons and keep more inmates in them longer. For that, funding is available, and for private prisons that businesses can make money from, since the incarcerated are the ones least likely to have political capital or voting power. In some states, voting rights are taken from prisoners once they are incarcerated, and where they are still allowed to vote, most prisoners are not aware that they have this right.

Racial and Ethnic Differences in Prison

My experience in prison also leads me to a racial and ethnic analysis of the motivation for keeping people incarcerated. When I say that prisons have become the contemporary manifestation of slavery, I do so with data to back up my assertion. Members of racial and ethnic minorities receive a disproportionate share of life sentences (Nellis and King, p. 2). Two-thirds of the people with life sentences are non-white—66.4 percent overall in the U.S. and a hard-to-believe 83.7 percent in New York! When we look at juveniles, we find that 77 percent of all youths sentenced to life in prison are members of ethnic and racial minorities. More black men are in prison now than lived under slavery during those dark days of American history.

When I walk through prisons, I am struck by the many young men of color inhabiting these horrific places. Usually, the guards are white, and the inmates are black or Latino—with the same true as well for incarcerated women. (In both cases, there is a smattering of female guards.) The racial disparity is obvious, and prisoners rail against the blatant racism, but their power is negligible and their often-poor families have little political clout. Thus, the number of minority group members rises, with little done about it and the disparities seldom pointed out except in studies and newspaper op-ed. It is time for the public to understand these issues and become more critical of the prison system and the sentencing of lifers inside the walls.

Clearly, some lifers in prison represent a continuing threat to society and should not be paroled, but they are in the minority. By incarcerating so many lifers who have changed, we are misusing the diminishing resources we as a society have available in times of economic crisis, and also disregarding people's ability to grow and mature. Parole boards and corrections professionals are more suited to determining eligibility than governors and other politicians whose decisions are based on political expediency and public opinion.

Aging in Prison

Another major issue with the lifer population is that many of them are now elderly, and although it was not intended that they spend the rest of their lives in prison, the reality is that the only way out for lifers often is in a coffin. Although the prosecutors' goal was not that they stay in prison for the rest of their lives, that is what is happening. In other parts of the world, such terms are unheard of, and in Western Europe, sentences of ten to fifteen years are considered quite long (http://www.nytimes.com/2005/10/02/national/02life.web.html?scp=2&sq=prison&st=nyt).

In 2006, an excellent study by the North Carolina Department of Correction's Division of Prisons looked at the aging inmate population to determine the severity of the problem and suggest solutions. It found that the population of elderly had increased faster than that of any other inmate age group over the previous twenty years. Because of the more-punitive response to crime nationally and the fact that the Baby Boomer generation now is becoming elderly, the number of prisoners over fifty in the state went up 61 percent, compared with 16 percent for the rest of the population. This has led to increased costs for medical and mental health services because of these prisoners' abuse of alcohol and other drugs, and poor preventative health care. They are now called the "early aging" population because their illnesses are similar to those of people who are at least ten years older in the general population (Price, 2006).

The health costs alone for housing inmates age fifty or older are almost four times those of younger inmates. In 2004 and 2005, the average cost of their health care—including medical, dental, and mental health—was $7,159, while for inmates under fifty, it was $1,919. Of the 245 prisoners over age fifty at six facilities that the study looked at, almost 25 percent were serving a life sentence, 58 percent had been in prison before, 74 percent were on medication and under medical care, 20 percent needed special diets, 55 percent believed that their medical conditions had declined since coming to prison, 29 percent needed special assistance like a cane, brace, or wheelchair, and 20 percent were receiving mental health care (p. 2). The researchers also found that most of the inmates over fifty were male, fifty-two percent were African-American, 47 percent were white, and the rest were Asian or Native American (p. 12).

As a result of this study, it was recommended that terminally ill inmates who were low security risks be released. Other suggestions were that elderly, ailing, and severely disabled inmates and those with special needs be sent to secure private facilities, and that legislation be considered to allow safe release into the community of more inmates with health issues (p. 3).

What was also useful about the study was that it included information from other states on what they did about the aged inmate population. Many states had only one or two small assisted-living facilities for elderly or disabled offenders. Some states had other specialized programs for the aged, including a minimum-custody assisted-living facility in Washington, a special-needs unit in Minnesota, and a skilled-nursing facility for the aged and mentally ill in Colorado. The Minnesota facility allowed those over fifty-five to opt out of participation in institutional programs if they saw themselves as "retired," and Pennsylvania had a number of programs for elderly inmates. The program in Pennsylvania, called STEP (Services to Elderly Prisoners), provided prerelease planning, parole planning, information on Social Security and Medicare, and social services for release and reintegration.

Ohio had one of the more progressive programs, with each prison offering services to inmates over fifty that included medication education, aid with memory loss, grandparenting discussions and lectures, and audiotaping of the inmate reading a children's book which is then sent to a family member. In addition, there are recreation programs, recovery programs, and aerobic exercise activities for the elderly. It is clear that some states are taking the aging of the inmate population seriously and thinking through how to integrate these people back into their communities or help them age with grace within the prisons. Such policy decisions need to be made in every state, and the sooner, the better.

Psychological Consequences of Long-Term Incarceration

Another great problem facing lifers and older people in prison is the long-term effects of incarceration on those who have been imprisoned for many years. The consequences of long-term incarceration have an impact on post-prison adjustment and make it harder for ex-prisoners to adapt to the outside world. Craig Haney, a psychologist at the University of California, Santa Cruz, has found that prison life has a detrimental effect on mental health even for people who are not mentally ill. He argues that adjusting to prisons has become even more difficult in the last several decades, that adapting to prison life exacts psychological costs, that some groups are more vulnerable to these incarceration costs, and that the psychological toll can make transition to the outside world harder (http://aspe.hhs.gov/hsp/prison2home02/Haney.htm 8/10/11).

Because of the rise in incarceration rates, American prisons are in crisis, with a U.S. rate that is consistently four to five times higher than those of Japan, the Netherlands, Australia, the United Kingdom, and other nations. As I have noted, we have abandoned most rehabilitation programs in prison, and violence has increased, especially because of the extent to which punitive approaches have been embraced.

As a result of longer sentences, those who are caught in the web of incarceration suffer greater psychological distress and long-term dysfunction. They are kept from the norms of living and interacting with the dominant society outside, and engage in a process of "prisonization"—shorthand for the negative psychological effects of a life behind bars. In other words, the norms of prison become the habits of thinking, feeling, and acting. These adaptations are natural but can become dysfunctional and counterproductive.

The longer a person is in prison, the more significant will be the institutional transformation. An example is the abandonment of privacy and liberty while being subjected to a lowering of status; one becomes stigmatized and learns that the sparse physical conditions of life will be stressful, unpleasant, and difficult (p. 4). Eventually, the transformation makes the inmate more accustomed to the restrictions that such a life imposes. He adjusts and begins to survive.

For younger people, the process is a bit easier, since many of them have not yet developed independent judgments and have little to revert to or rely on. But the longer one remains in prison, the more the process will change them, not always for the better. The sense of dependence on the institutional structure that often develops can cause a muting of initiative and independence. Giving up day-to-day control over their decisions leads inmates to rely on the structure to decide how they will organize themselves.

In addition, inmates are structured in their behaviors by external controls that others define which immerse them in a network of rules and regulations. They learn to live by such rules, and when they are taken away, the prisoners find that they do not always know what to do on their own. Recently, an inmate who had done thirty years told me he was amazed at the lack of civility in the outside society. He had for so long behaved respectfully of other inmates, as required in prison, that he was chagrined to see how mean people on the outside could be to each other.

He described a situation in which the driver behind the car he was riding in became consumed by road rage, and the driver of his car, rather than ignore it, responded the same way; the ex-prisoner was worried that the altercation would become violent, unlike anything he had experienced in prison. He couldn't decide what to do in such a situation because he was used to rules and regulations that included treating each other respectfully and allowing others their personal space. This was out of his realm of experience.

The process of prisonization can also lead to hypervigilance, distrust, and suspicion. Inmates must be ever-alert to signs of threat and personal risk, and learn to project a tough convict veneer; they do not want to be dominated or exploited during their incarceration. Usually, it is the younger men who project that tough image to protect themselves. The older prisoners have earned respect by virtue of their years inside and ability to survive.

Some prisoners learn to become socially isolated and withdrawn. By being inconspicuous and unobtrusive, they can be off the radar and end up leading lives of quiet desperation. Because this isn't dealt with, it often can look like clinical depression. Some prisoners are humorless and become flat in their responses. Others experience an existential death, remaining cut off and alone (Haney, p. 7).

Some sets of prisoners might become exploitative of others, learning to dominate and control their fellow inmates as a response to feeling exploited themselves. If there are no meaningful programs to teach more pro-social behaviors, prisoners can resort to dangerous activities to seek intimacy and connection. This hyper-masculinity is not uncommon in prison, often among younger inmates who have no models for more-human expressions of intimacy. Instead, aggression and violence become conflated with ideas of intimacy as a prisoner tries to make his way in the system. He might have learned this behavior at home or on the street, and thinks it is the way to "make it" in prison.

Other prisoners might begin to have a diminished sense of self-worth, especially as they are denied basic privacy rights. Prisoners live in cramped and deteriorating spaces, often the size of a king-sized bed and shared with another "cellie." They have no choice over when they go to bed, eat, or take most other actions in their lives. They may come to feel infantilized and stigmatized, and some can eventually internalize these ideas, feeling that they deserve this kind of treatment because of who they are.

Recently at San Quentin, a group of older, relatively mellow lifers was moved to another cellblock that they were forced to share with inmates newly processed to the prison—young, trouble-making hotheads and gang-bangers. In addition, the cellblock they were moved to was filled with mold, the cells had little electricity, and there were no hot showers. Most of the lifers, who were used to being in their own group in better conditions than this, nevertheless put up with the horrific situation until a few rebelled and spoke out to the prison administration. Outsiders tried to make a difference, and public health officials came in to investigate, leading to a few small changes in how the inmates were treated. Prison activism does take place, often by those who are more outspoken and aware that their human rights have been violated, but usually, there is little result.

Finally, there are post-traumatic reactions to the physical and mental pains of being incarcerated. If people have been victims of child abuse, poverty, or maltreatment, their social histories lead to revictimization behind bars. The powerlessness of being in prison reminds the inmate of that childhood powerlessness, and even those who appear normal on the outside carry the scars for a lifetime. This post-traumatic reaction can be hidden until they leave the relative "safety" of the prison which had kept them controlled, directed, and balanced. Sometimes, prison has been a harbor in an otherwise-chaotic world. Being paroled and leaving a prison, although hoped for and sought, can trigger a mental health crisis.

The psychological consequences of incarceration can lead to a range of troubles after parole. Even the healthiest prisoners face transition troubles. Recently, a prisoner who had been inside for twenty-nine years told me he was not informed of his discharge until 5 p.m. on the day of his parole. The agency that was going to take responsibility for him was already closed for the day and so could not come for him. Instead, the prison system had him put his personal belongings in two garbage bags and brought him to the gate, where he was left to fend for himself. It was 8 p.m., and he had nowhere to go. He is a mentally healthy, sixty-nine-year-old man, and was freaked out. Luckily, another prisoner was being paroled at the same time, and his driver took the elderly man to a homeless shelter for a bed until the next day, when he connected with the agency he was going to live with.

Transition from prison to home is, at best, a challenging experience. If one has mental health issues after years of incarceration, the transition is even more difficult. There is little evidence that prisons across the country have responded to the psychological issues related to incarceration (Haney, p. 10). When inmates are let out of prison, many take their psychological trauma with them. Some reenter their families with diminished ability to deal with parenting and family life. The hypervigilance and alienation that others developed inside also can make going home problematic.

One must be authentic in a family, as well as emotionally honest. Little to help gain these skills is taught in prison unless one has access to the kind of programming that is not available in most prisons. Typical is the inmate who went home after twenty-three years inside and found that his attempts to reassert his male authority were not well received by a wife and family that had adapted to his absence; it took quite a while for them to find an equilibrium. Work on transition issues before his release would have helped him adjust more quickly and smoothly.

Haney has noted that the large number of imprisoned black men has become a significant factor in the breakdown of the African-American family. It has led to the disruption of family life, the prevalence of single-parent families, and children being raised without a father in the home. This leads to the inability of both those who grow up in such homes and the prisoners themselves when they're released to get what few jobs are still available (Haney, p. 11).

International Comparisons

We can see clearly from Haney's work that little has been done to deal with the psychological impact of incarceration and its long-term effects on our society. Other countries have done better. For example, most of Europe is now a death penalty-free zone because of the movement away from capital punishment (Coyle, p. 1). About half of all prisoners in the world are in the U.S., Russia, and China, which have about a quarter of the total population (Walmsley, 2003). The U.S. has the highest prison population rate in the world: 686 per 100,000.

In most countries, the majority of convicted prisoners are serving comparatively shorter sentences than in the U.S. (Coyle, p. 3). In Scandinavian countries, for example, anyone serving more than six months is viewed as a long-term prisoner. In the United Kingdom, early release is considered for anyone who has served four years. The Council of Europe considers long-term prisoners those who have served five years or more. Compare that to the U.S., where prisoners can serve twenty, thirty, or forty years. In Spain, the maximum sentence for *any* crime is thirty years, and those are determinate sentences; the prisoners know when they will get out—unlike our policies in the U.S.

Not only do we incarcerate people for longer periods and have high rates of incarceration but we also have harsher sentences for crimes that receive less time in other countries. For example, burglars in the U.S. serve an average of 16.2 months in prison, compared with 5.3 months in Canada and 6.8 months in England and Wales (Maurer, 2003).

The reasons for these differences lie in the sentencing policies of the countries, not the severity of the crimes, which are quite similar internationally, Maurer notes. For example, when Finland became concerned in the 1970s about its growing prison population compared with the rest of Scandinavia, it instituted a series of policy reforms involving more suspended sentences and earlier eligibility for parole. Consequently, the rate of incarceration declined by 40 percent from 1976 to 1992 (p. 9).

In Germany, prison admissions were reduced by decreasing the use of short sentences, which were found to do more harm than good by disrupting the offenders' ties to their communities and making them part of a prison subculture that led to stigmatization (p. 9). In Russia, an amnesty because of the terrible conditions in prison and long pretrial detentions led to a sharp decline in the incarcerated population as prisoners were released to control costs and overcrowding (p. 10).

The reputation of the U.S. criminal justice system internationally is deplorable (p. 11). Many countries in Europe are moving toward rehabilitation while the U.S. is notorious for its lack of rehabilitation programs in prisons. Canada is working toward a new policy of evaluating prisoners for early parole release, and in France, a commission created because of publicity about inhumane conditions has recommended that a broad range of rights be granted to prisoners.

The racial trends are similar to those in the U.S., with minorities having the highest rates of incarceration in Australia, Canada, England, and Wales. In Canada, it is the native population whose rate is eight times higher than that of non-natives, and in Australia, Aboriginals are fifteen times more likely to be incarcerated (p. 11).

As has been found in the U.S., prisoners with life sentences are the least likely to be dangerous and reoffend in other countries as well (Coyle, p. 3). They have better disciplinary records than those serving shorter sentences, and often are seen as stabilizing influences in the prison population (p. 3). In England and Wales, just 9 percent of 1,587 life-sentence prisoners released in the period from 1972 to 1994 were reconvicted, compared with the 57 percent of all prisoners discharged in 1996 who were reconvicted within two years (p. 3).

Policy Recommendations

With all this being said, there are a few policy recommendations that could easily be enacted and would dramatically change the lives of prisoners, especially lifers—as well as save the taxpayers much money in a difficult time.

First and foremost, we need to find a way to reduce the population of elderly prisoners. As the data shows, these people rarely cause trouble and cost an enormous amount to house and treat. By paroling them to elder-care facilities geared to treating the formerly incarcerated, we both become more humane and save money. In addition:

• Allow the parole system to work. Rather than having a politicized system in which every administration has another approach to incarceration, let those who have evaluated prisoners for years determine if someone is ready.

• Make the parole system more clear, and those who determine suitability more equitable in dealing with inmates. In the current politicized system, every administration has another idea on methods and standards for parole. Often, parole board members change the rules every time a prisoner appears before them. The boards should be determining whether the inmate is a danger and how well an individual has responded to institutional programs. For those who have not done well, the list of what needs to be accomplished by the next hearing should be spelled out clearly. And an inmate who meets the criteria should be judged suitable for parole and scheduled for release. In other words, end the arbitrary nature of the parole process.

• Prepare prisoners for parole. Rather than spending so much money on warehousing people, use the same funds for programming inside prison walls that can ready the inmates for the real world. Teach computer skills; talk about finances, finding a job and a place to live, and reintegration into families. Provide help with the psychological effects of long-term incarceration rather than just putting people out with $200 in their pockets and a nod of goodbye.

• Rethink the life-without-parole option. Although it seemed like a good alternative to the death penalty, there might be other ways of solving the problem that do not keep thousands of human beings locked away for the rest of their lives.

• Provide Pell Grants and other financial aid to students in prison so they can educate and rehabilitate themselves in preparation for release. This will allow more educational programs to flourish inside and reduce recidivism rates significantly.

• Repeal the three-strikes law which is incarcerating people who have not committed violent felonies, and begin to rethink how to handle nonviolent offenders.

• Make more rehabilitation programs available for inmates of all U.S. prisons, not just the few select institutions near urban centers where volunteers are available.

• Work on restorative justice and alternatives to incarceration as ways of dealing with people who commit crimes.

Although there are many more solutions to the issues raised in this book, I fear that most will not be considered or even put on any policy-maker's agenda. Nonetheless, I hope I have raised the awareness of a concerned population that might further explore the issues I have highlighted here. I am merely a person trying to do a little good in the world, trying to right some wrongs that I have encountered along my path.

Some people may think I am naïve and a "bleeding heart liberal." But I have seen what I've described to you with my own eyes, and I want to educate others about these horrific situations. We should no longer turn a blind eye to the pain and suffering that goes on daily in the prisons that most of us never think about. I urge you to look behind those walls, think of the lives in there, and remember that "prisoners are people, too."

In Conclusion

As you might remember, I said at the beginning of this book that I was drawn to the dark side of people's lives. When I entered the darkness of prison life, I had no idea of the light and personal growth it would lead to. I also had no idea that I would touch the lives of others and bring some light to their darkness. Nor did I know that the prisoners would give my own life such significance and power. That is probably the most profound part of doing this kind of work. Rather than close with a simple few sentences of conclusion, I want to end with a poem written one day in our New Leaf on Life group by a prisoner who was prompted to explore poetry by a writing workshop professor. I believe it sums up well what we as citizens need to know about lifers and other prisoners who are kept from our eyes and consciousness. I hope it can help lead us to the important actions that must be taken, and to understand that there is light within the darkness of prisons:

I am a son of automobile makers, farmers,
Homemakers, entrepreneurs,
Landowners, musicians, general laborers

I have seen my father's destiny
Expand and contract
Weighted down by his obligations
Through procreation, becoming untangled and
   rearranged
In a simplistic modification of peace

I have heard my mother's prayers,
For more time, more help
And more wisdom in handling
Her day to day responsibilities

I am me, modest and humble
An ex-rebel, more spirited
With a waiting attitude in which
To be complete. I see myself
Stagnated awaiting redemption by
The secular authorities, waiting
For my turn for life. My needs
Are no longer shaped by worldly
Desire, they are now
Shaped by what I need to
Survive while remaining true
To my God.

— Ray, personal communication

Sources

American Council on Education. "Higher Education Behind Bars: Postsecondary Prison Education Programs Make a Difference." http://www.acenet/edu/AM/Template.cfm?Section-Homes& TEMPLATE-/cm/ContentDisp. 6/2/11.

Coley, R. and P. Barton. Educational Testing Service. "Locked Up and Locked Out: An Educational Perspective on the U.S. Prison Population." Policy Information Report. March 2006.

Coyle, Andrew. "Management of Long-Term and Life-Sentence Prisoners Internationally in the Context of a Human Rights Strategy." www.westminster.ac.uk/fb-mirror/cache.cgi.

Dannenberg, John E. "U.S. Supreme Court: California's Prison Overcrowding Violates Eighth Amendment; Must Be Remediated by Prison Reduction." Prison Legal News, July, 2011.

Dannenberg, John E. "U.S. Supreme Court: Federal Habeas Relief Disallowed for California Lifer Parole Denials." Prison Legal News, January 2011.

Dannenberg, John E. "The Non-Adversarial Lifer Parole System." California Lifer Newsletter #42, February, 2012.

Davis, Angela. Are Prisons Obsolete? New York: Seven Stories Press. 2003.

Egelko, Bob. "Life With Parole Found to be Usually a 20-Year Term." San Francisco Chronicle. 9/16/11.

Gehring, Thom. "The History of Correctional Education." Correctional Education Association. http://www.ceanational.org/abouttce/history.htm. 6/25/07.

Granoff, Gillian. "Schools Behind Bars: Prison College Programs Unlock the Keys to Human Potential." Education Online Update. http:/www.educationupdate.com/archives/2005/May/html. 6/2/11.

Haney, Craig. "The Psychological Impact of Incarceration: Implications for Post-Prison Adjustment." December, 2001. http://aspe.hhs.gov/hsp/prison2home02/Haney.htm. 8/10/11.

Irwin, John. Lifers: Seeking Redemption in Prison. New York: Routledge. 2009.

Lagos, Marisa. "Bill Would Raise Bar on Parole for Lifers." San Francisco Chronicle. 8/29/11.

Lindblom, Charles. "Still Muddling, Not Yet Through." Public Administration Review. November/December, 1979.

McCarty, Heather Jane. "Educating Felons: Reflections on Higher Education in Prison." Radical History Review. Issue 96. Fall, 2006.

Mauer, Marc. "Comparative International Rates of Incarceration: An Examination of Causes and Trends. Presented to the U.S. Commission on Civil Rights." June 20, 2003. The Sentencing Project.

Moore, Solomon. "Number of Life Terms Hits Record." New York Times. 9/23/09.

Mullane, Nancy. Life After Murder: Five Men in Search of Redemption. Public Affairs. 2012.

Mullane, Nancy. "Governor Brown Takes 180 Degree Turn on Parole for Lifers." KLAW News. 5/26/11.

Nahmias, Rick. Golden States of Grace: Prayers of the Disinherited. Albuquerque: University of New Mexico Press. 2010.

Nellis, Ashley and Ryan S. King. "No Exit: The Expanding Use of Life Sentences in America." July, 2009. The Sentencing Project.

New York Times. 9/13/11.

New York Times. 7/19/11.

Price, Charlotte A. "Aging Inmate Population Study." North Carolina Department of Correction Division of Prisons. May, 2006.

Prison University Project. http://www.prisonuniversity project. org/about/about-us.html. 6/2/11.

San Francisco Chronicle. 9/16/11.

Steurer, Stephen, Linda Smith and Alice Tracy (2001). "Three-State Recidivism Study." Correctional Education Association. Lanham, MD.

Walmsley, Roy. "World Prison Population List (4th edition)." Findings 188 Home Office, Crown 2003.

Wetherbee, Winthrop. "Cornell at Auburn: An Experiment in Teaching and Learning." http://cuauburn.arts.cornell.edu/ wetherbee.html. 6/25/07.

Wright, J. (editor). The New York Times Almanac: The Almanac of Record. New York: Penguin Reference. 2006.

Wright, Randall. "Going to Teach in Prison: Culture Shock." Journal of Correctional Education. March, 2005.

Essays by Prisoners

Baylor, Don. "Personal Story." Fall, 2011.

Black. "Mystory: A Public Education Experience." 6/8/11.

Great Mind. "Personal Story." 2006.

Jinryu. "Personal Story." Fall, 2011.

Little Man. "A Letter of Forgiveness for my Past." Fall, 2011.

Mike. "Personal Story." Fall, 2011.

Moishe. "Personal Story." Fall, 2011.

Phylo. "Personal Story." Fall, 2011.

Savio. "Personal Story." Fall, 2011.

Yohannan. "Personal Story." Fall, 2011.

Essays by Students

Coyne, Heather. Personal Essay. Spring, 2011.

Dickinson, Taylor. Personal Essay. Spring, 2011.

Keegan, Claire. Personal Remembrance of Visit to San Quentin. Fall, 2011.

Essays by Professors

Dr. Cynthia Boaz

Dr. Lynn Cominsky

Dr. Diana Grant

Dr. Amy Kittelstrom

Dr. Rick Luttman

Dr. Eric Williams

Essays by Teaching Assistants and Private Citizens

John Kelly

Dr. Jody Short and Dr. Elizabeth Durgin. 3/4/04

About the Author

Dr. Elaine Leeder, MSW, MPH, PhD, is a Professor of Sociology and Dean of the School of Social Sciences at Sonoma State University in Rohnert Park, CA. Previously, she was a Professor at Ithaca College in Ithaca, NY. She has thirty-five years of distinguished accomplishments and experience in academia and public service.

Leeder is listed in Who's Who of American Women, Who's Who in America, and Who's Who of American Teachers. Her career encompasses roles as professor/teacher, psychotherapist, consultant, author, and advocate for social justice. Awards include a National Endowment for the Humanities Fellowship, outstanding teaching awards, research and travel grants, and numerous awards from student and community agencies. She was a visiting scholar at the U.S. Holocaust Memorial Museum in Washington, DC. Twice, she sailed on the University of Pittsburgh's Semester at Sea, once serving as Core Director to all seven hundred passengers on board, and has appeared on Road Rules on MTV in conjunction with the voyage.

She received her undergraduate degree from Northeastern University, master's in social work from New York's Wurzweiler School of Social Work at Yeshiva University, and a master's in public health from the University of California School of Public Health in Berkeley. She completed her doctoral work at Cornell University in 1985. Over the years, she has published four other books and more than two dozen articles on sociological and psychological issues. Her third book, *The Family in Global Perspective: A Gendered Journey*, is being used at dozens of campuses in the U.S. today. Leeder lives in Sebastopol, CA, and travels widely.